CW00961729

EGON RONAY'S
GUIDE
TO THE
LAKE DISTRICT
AND
YORKSHIRE
DALES

Establishment research conducted by a team of full-time professional inspectors, who are trained to achieve common standards of judgement with as much objectivity as this field allows. Their professional identities are not disclosed until they seek information from the management after paying their bills. The Guide is independent in its editorial selection and does not accept advertising, payment or hospitality from the establishments covered.

Egon Ronay's Guides
Second Floor, Greencoat House,
Francis Street, London SW1P 1DH

Head of Editorial Moyra Fraser
Editor Michèle Roche
Chief copywriter Peter Long
Editorial contributors Margaret Armstrong
                          Joy Langridge
Publisher William Halden

Cover design Carole Thomas & Associates
Cover illustration Shirley Trevena
Illustrator Pat Thorne
Page design Suzanne Sykes

Photographs from the AA Photo Library unless otherwise stated.

Maps produced by the Cartographic Department of the Automobile Association.

The contents of this book are believed correct at the time of printing. Nevertheless, the publisher can accept no responsibility for errors or omissions or changes in the details given.

© The Automobile Association 1987
All rights reserved. No part of this publication may be reproduced, stored in a retrieval system or transmitted in any form or by any means – electronic, mechanical, photocopying, recording or otherwise – unless the written permission of the publisher has been given beforehand.

Distributed in the United Kingdom by the Publishing Division of The Automobile Association, Fanum House, Basingstoke, Hampshire RG21 2EA and overseas by the British Tourist Authority, Thames Tower, Black's Road, London W6 9EL

ISBN 0 86145 507 X
AA Ref 51978

Printed & bound in Great Britain by William Clowes, Beccles, Suffolk
Typeset by Tradespools Limited, Frome, Somerset

CONTENTS

HOW TO USE THIS GUIDE

ORDER OF LISTINGS
Establishments are listed in alphabetical order by location within two sections: Cumbria & Lake District
Yorkshire Dales

MAP REFERENCES
Map references are to the map section at the front of the book or to a town/area plan printed with the entries.

PRICES
Accommodation
We print categories from A–F rather than actual prices. These are based on the current price, including VAT (also service if applicable), for a double room for two occupants with private bath and cooked breakfast. *PUB (B & B)* prices, however, may not always include private bath.

£ A over £110
£ B £85 to £110
£ C £65 to £85
£ D £50 to £65
£ E £35 to £50
£ F under £35

Where our calculations show the price to be just above or below the borderline between two categories we symbolise the price as, for example, £ C/D.

Food
About £ . . . for two indicates the approximate cost in a *RES-TAURANT* of a three-course meal including wine, coffee, service and VAT. This is based on a choice from average-priced dishes on the menu and includes one of the least expensive bottles of wine.

Where set menus are offered this is denoted by Set L or Set D, followed by their respective prices.

Two **typical prices** are listed, valid at the time of our visit, for each *JUST A BITE* and *PUB (FOOD)* entry. Minimum charges per person are indicated within Just a Bite entries, as establishments in this categories often choose to employ a minimum charge during busy periods.

GRADING
Hotels
According to their percentage rating, hotels are classified as

De luxe 85–100%
Grade 1 70–84%
Grade 2 50–69%

The percentage shown on a hotel entry is an individual rating arrived at after careful testing, inspection and calculation according to our unique grading system. The size of the hotels and the prices charged are not considered in the grading, nor is the food. **If we recommend meals in a hotel or inn, a separate entry is made for its dining room.**

Inns
These are not graded. We distinguish them from hotels by their more modest nature, usually with respect to the day rooms. For our purposes, an inn is normally either a pub with hotel-style accommodation or a small hotel with a bar and the atmosphere of a pub.

Restaurants
  ★ We award one to three stars for excellence of cooking. One star
 ★★ represents cooking much above average, two stars outstanding
★★★ cooking, and three the best in the land.

We only include restaurants where the cooking comes up to our minimum standards, however attractive the place may be in other respects. We take into account how well the restaurant achieves what it sets out to do as reflected in the menu, decor, prices, publicity, atmosphere – factors that add up to some of the expectation.

Just a Bite
★ Food much above average

A team of professional inspectors conduct a nationwide quest for 'Just a Bite', seeking high-quality food at modest prices and selecting only those establishments which meet their rigorous standards of excellence. They avoid full restaurant meals in the traditional sense, concentrating instead on afternoon teas, fish and chips, snacks and inexpensive meals at bistros, wine bars, cafés, etc. Large chain caterers are not included.

Pubs
★ Bar food much above average

We only include establishments where our team of inspectors found excellent-quality bar food.

Some pubs are recommended for *ATMOSPHERE* only.

SYMBOLS

♀	A house wine that is judged well chosen by our inspectors
⌒	An outstanding wine list
⊛	A good cheeseboard
☕	Spotlights Just a Bite establishments recommended for good tea
WC	As washroom facilities are sometimes limited in the type of establishment within our Just a Bite category, we use this to indicate where a clean lavatory with soap, towels, paper and running water was found
(Food)	Pubs recommended for bar food
(B & B)	Pubs recommended for accommodation
Check-in	If residents can check in to pubs for accommodation at any time, we print all day; if check-in is restricted, as the publican's free time is traditionally in the afternoon, when he or she is sometimes not available, we print restricted.
Family Pubs	Those pubs we suggest as suitable for families (children welcome) are ones that have a room or indoor area where children are allowed whether eating or not. Many pubs will only welcome children if they are eating.
Beers	After Beers we list a selection (or all) of the beers currently available, including lagers and cider on draught. Real ale appears if any of the beers can be defined as such. Additionally, immediately before this information, we indicate whether an establishment is a free house or brewery-owned.

RESTRICTIONS

Any restrictions on children, dogs, smoking, licensing, and limited choice on availability of fare during certain periods, is printed at the end of each entry. It should be noted, however, that many establishments remain flexible on some issues and we only print restrictions for those establishments which have a definite policy in these matters. Many Just a Bite establishments have flexible opening hours because of their small size or remote location and it is therefore advisable to check. It should also be noted that pub opening hours vary throughout the country. Some pubs have a six-day licence. Again it is advisable to check, particularly during Christmas and the New Year.

NOW ALSO AVAILABLE

IN THE
Egon Ronay's Guide
SERIES

THE

1987 PUB GUIDE

TO BAR FOOD AND ACCOMMODATION IN BRITISH PUBS AND INNS

The best British bar snacks and meals
☐
Highly selective
☐
Surprising gastronomic finds at low prices
☐
Pubs that welcome children
☐
Homely, clean and pleasant bedrooms
☐
Excellent breakfasts

**Available from AA Centres
and booksellers everywhere at £4.95
or £5.95 including postage
and packing from:**

**Mail Order Department
PO Box 51
Basingstoke
Hampshire
RG21 2BR**

·S·E·N·D·F·O·R·Y·O·U·R·C·O·P·Y·N·O·W·

Hide & Seek

Spirit of Grasmere, bells of Ambleside,
Sing you and ring you, water bells, for me;
You water-colour waterfalls may froth.
Long hiking holidays will yet provide
Long stony lanes and back at six to tea
And Heinz's ketchup on the tablecloth.

John Betjeman wrote "Lake District" in 1958 and our inspectors might well have echoed this as they researched this book. The Lakes have for many years enjoyed a reputation for good food, but on closer inspection those heavenly shrouds of mist across the lakes and fells provided a smokescreen for dozens of mediocre, if not downright disgraceful, eating places. It is not insignificant that Kendal has just erected a vast edifice to American fast food.

As these favourite tourist areas are dominated by natural beauty, one would expect to discover a wealth of lovely country inns or tea shops. Well, you can find them but in too many much of the food is most unlovely. The packet, can opener, deep-fryer and microwave still dominate. Basket meals, monosodium glutamate soups and pappy sandwiches are still too often the dishes of the day.

Even the splendid country house hotels on both sides of the M6 motorway, which once set the standard for so many, have lost some of their sparkle. Flashes of stardom can still be seen but long years of renown and continually increasing popularity have brought a degree of complacency.

Tradition in the Lakes and Dales is so overpowering that food can be turned into lucrative tourist attractions with just the addition of the word "Famous" or "Original". Yet we had to search the olde-worlde towns long and hard to locate any traditional grocers and bakers among the supermarkets or discover good local food stalls in the markets. All is not lost however. In Kendal we found one of the finest cheese stalls you could hope for: witness Peter Gott in the market hall on Saturdays.

But as you can see from the pages of this book, our search for excellence was eventually rewarded with over 200 recommended establishments. And to echo the words of William Wordsworth, that most famous of Lakeland poets: "Pleasures newly found are sweet". May that also be your experience. . .

William Halden, Publisher

STARRED ESTABLISHMENTS

RESTAURANTS
ONE STAR

Grasmere, Cumbria: White Moss House Restaurant
Ilkley, West Yorkshire: Box Tree Restaurant
Pool-in-Wharfedale, West Yorkshire: Pool Court
Ullswater, Cumbria: Sharrow Bay Hotel Restaurant

JUST A BITE

Ambleside, Cumbria: Rothay Manor Lounge
Ambleside, Cumbria: Sheila's Cottage
Barden, North Yorkshire: Low House Farm
Bolton Abbey, North Yorkshire: Bolton Abbey Tea Cottage
Borrowdale, Cumbria: Lodore Swiss Hotel Lounge
Cockermouth, Cumbria: Quince & Medlar
Melmerby, Cumbria: Village Bakery
Skipton, North Yorkshire: Herbs Wholefood & Vegetarian Restaurant
Ullswater, Cumbria: Sharrow Bay Hotel Lounge

PUBS

Kirkby Stephen, Cumbria: King's Arms Hotel
Moulton, North Yorkshire: Black Bull Inn

DE LUXE AND GRADE 1 HOTELS

80% Ullswater, Cumbria: Sharrow Bay Hotel
79% Grasmere, Cumbria: Michael's Nook
77% Bolton Abbey, North Yorkshire: Devonshire Arms Hotel
Borrowdale, Cumbria: Lodore Swiss Hotel
76% Kirkby Fleetham, North Yorkshire: Kirkby Fleetham Hall
75% Ullswater, Cumbria: Leeming on Ullswater
74% Langdale, Cumbria: Pillar Hotel
73% Windermere, Cumbria: Miller Howe Hotel
72% Brampton, Cumbria: Farlam Hall Hotel
Grasmere, Cumbria: Wordsworth Hotel
Harrogate, North Yorkshire: Majestic Hotel
71% Ambleside, Cumbria: Rothay Manor
Jervaulx, North Yorkshire: Jervaulx Hall
Markington, North Yorkshire: Hob Green Hotel

BEAUTIFULLY SITUATED HOTELS

Many regions of the British Isles are renowned for their scenic beauty, and for hotels in these areas, the setting and views are often among their most important attributes. The following is a list of hotels judged by our inspectors to be beautifully situated.

CUMBRIA & LAKES

Ambleside: Rothay Manor
Bassenthwaite: Armathwaite Hall
Borrowdale: Borrowdale Hall
Borrowdale: Lodore Swiss Hotel
Brampton: Farlam Hall Hotel
Cartmel: Aynsome Manor Hotel
Crosby-on-Eden: Crosby Lodge
Grasmere: Michael's Nook
Grizedale: Grizedale Lodge Hotel
Keswick: Underscar Hotel
Troutbeck: Mortal Man
Ullswater: Leeming on Ullswater
Ullswater: Old Church Hotel
Ullswater: Rampsbeck Hotel
Underbarrow: Greenriggs Country House

Windermere: Langdale Chase Hotel
Windermere: Miller Howe Hotel

YORKSHIRE DALES

Jervaulx: Jervaulx Hall Hotel
Kirkby Fleetham: Kirkby Fleetham Hall
Otley: Chevin Lodge

COUNTRY HOUSE HOTELS

This is a select category of small hotels offering civilised comfort, good service and fine food in an attractive and peaceful rural setting. Most of them are imposing country mansions, converted and run with loving care by dedicated owners, often a husband-and-wife team. None of them has more than 30 bedrooms; all have recommended in-house restaurants.

CUMBRIA & LAKES

Brampton, Cumbria: Farlam Hall Hotel
Grasmere, Cumbria: Michael's Nook
Ullswater, Cumbria: Sharrow Bay Hotel
Windermere, Cumbria: Miller Howe Hotel

YORKSHIRE DALES

Kildwick, North Yorkshire: Kildwick Hall
Kirkby Fleetham, North Yorkshire, Kirkby Fleetham Hall

HOTELS WITH SWIMMING POOLS

INDOOR

CUMBRIA & LAKES

Bassenthwaite: Armathwaite
Borrowdale: Lodore Swiss
Bowness on Windermere: Belsfield
Carlisle: Ladbroke Crown & Mitre
Carlisle: Swallow Hilltop
Grasmere: Wordsworth
Langdale: Pillar

YORKSHIRE DALES

Harrogate: Majestic
Harrogate: St. George

OUTDOOR

CUMBRIA & LAKES

Borrowdale: Lodore Swiss
Bowness on Windermere: Old England

FISHING

CUMBRIA & LAKES

Ambleside: Nanny Brow
Ambleside: Wateredge
Bassenthwaite: Armathwaite
Crooklands: Crooklands
Grasmere: White Moss House
Keswick: Underscar
Langdale: Pillar
Newby Bridge: Swan
Ullswater: Leeming on Ullswater
Ullswater: Old Church
Ullswater: Rampsbeck
Ullswater: Sharrow Bay

YORKSHIRE DALES

Bolton Abbey: Devonshire Arms
Otley: Chevin Lodge
Threshfield: Wilson Arms

TENNIS

CUMBRIA & LAKES

Bassenthwaite: Armathwaite Hall
Borrowdale: Lodore Swiss
Bowness on Windermere: Belsfield
Windermere: Langdale Chase

YORKSHIRE DALES

Harrogate: Majestic
Harrogate: Old Swan
Ilkley: Craiglands

SQUASH

CUMBRIA & LAKES

Bassenthwaite: Armathwaite Hall
Borrowdale: Lodore Swiss
Langdale: Pillar

YORKSHIRE DALES

Harrogate: Majestic

OPEN AIR EATING

CUMBRIA & LAKES

Alston, Brownside Coach House
Ambleside, Rothay Manor
Ambleside, Zeffirellis
Appleby-in-Westmorland, Royal Oak Inn
Askham, Punch Bowl
Bassenthwaite Lake, Pheasant Inn
Boot, Brook House
Borrowdale, Lodore Swiss Hotel Lounge
Bowness on Windermere, Jackson's Bistro
Bowness on Windermere, Laurel Cottage
Bowness on Windermere, Porthole Eating House
Bowness on Windermere, Trattoria Pizzeria Ticino

Braithwaite, Book Cottage
Brampton, Tarn End
Carlisle, Hudson's Coffee Shop
Cartmel Fell, Mason's Arms
Clifton Dykes, Wetheriggs Pottery Centre, Schofield's
Coniston, Bridge House Café
Dodd Wood, Old Sawmill
Eskdale Green, Bower House Inn
Faugh, String of Horses
Grange-in-Borrowdale, Grange Bridge Cottage
Grange-over-Sands, At Home
Grasmere, Coffee Bean
Grasmere, Michael's Nook Restaurant
Grasmere, Rowan Tree
Grizedale, Grizedale Lodge, Restaurant in the Forest
High Lorton, White Ash Barn
Kendal, Moon
Kendal, Nutters
Kendal, Waterside Wholefoods
Kents Bank, Abbot Hall Coffee Shop
Keswick, Dog & Gun
Keswick, Pheasant Inn
Keswick, Underscar Hotel
Langdale, Pillar Hotel, Hobson's Pub
Little Langdale, Three Shires
Lowick Green, Farmers Arms

Melmerby, Shepherds Inn
Penrith, Bluebell Tearoom
Rockcliffe, Crown & Thistle
Sandside, Ship Inn
Talkin Village, Hare & Hounds Inn
Troutbeck, Mortal Man Hotel
Ullswater, Leeming on Ullswater Restaurant
Wasdale Head, Wasdale Head Inn
Windermere, Langdale Chase Hotel Lounge
Windermere, Miller Howe Hotel Lounge

YORKSHIRE DALES

Barden, Howgill Lodge
Bolton Abbey, Bolton Abbey Tea Cottage
Constable Burton, Wyvill Arms
Dent, Dent Crafts Centre
Hawes, Cockett's Hotel
Kettlewell, Racehorses Hotel
Kildwick, Kidwick Hall, Candle Lite Room
Kirkby Stephen, King's Arms Hotel
Moulton, Black Bull Inn
Otley, Chatters Tea Shoppe
Sutton Howgrave, White Dog Inn
Wath-in-Nidderdale, Sportsman's Arms

11

SUNDAY EATING

CUMBRIA & LAKES

Alston, Brownside Coach House

Ambleside, Harvest

Ambleside, Kirkstone Foot Hotel

Ambleside, Rothay Manor Restaurant & Lounge

Ambleside, Zeffirellis

Appleby, Royal Oak Inn

Askham, Punch Bowl

Bassenthwaite Lake, Pheasant Inn (L)

Boot, Brook House Restaurant

Borrowdale, Lodore Swiss Hotel Restaurant & Lounge

Bowness on Windermere, Hedgerow

Bowness on Windermere, Jackson's Bistro

Bowness on Windermere, Laurel Cottage

Bowness on Windermere, Porthole Eating House

Bowness on Windermere, Trattoria Pizzeria Ticino

Braithwaite, Book Cottage

Brampton, Farlam Hall Hotel Restaurant (D)

Brampton, Tarn End

Caldeck, Swaledale Watch

Cartmel, St. Mary's Lodge

Cartmel, Uplands

Cartmel Fell, Mason's Arms

Clifton Dykes, Wetheriggs Pottery Centre, Schofield's

Cockermouth, Wythop Mill

Coniston, Bridge House Café

Crosby-on-Eden, Crosby Lodge Hotel Restaurant

Dodd Wood, Old Sawmill

Eskdale Green, Bower House Inn

Faugh, String of Horses

Grange-in-Borrowdale, Grange Bridge Cottage

Grasmere, Baldry's

Grasmere, Coffee Bean

Grasmere, Michael's Nook

Grasmere, Rowan Tree

Grasmere, Wordsworth Hotel, Prelude Restaurant

Grizedale, Grizedale Lodge, Restaurant in the Forest

Hawkshead, Field Head House Restaurant

Hawkshead, Minstrel's Gallery

Hawkshead, Queen's Head

High Lorton, White Ash Barn

Kendal, Moon

Kents Bank, Abbot Hall Coffee Shop

Keswick, Dog & Gun

Keswick, Mayson's

Keswick, Squire's

Keswick, Underscar Hotel Lounge

Langdale, Pillar Hotel, Hobson's Pub

Little Langdale, Three Shires Inn

Lowick Green, Farmer's Arms

Melmerby, Shepherds Inn

Melmerby, Village Bakery

Penrith, Passepartout (June–Sept)

Rockcliffe, Crown & Thistle (L)

Sparkbridge, Bridgefield House Restaurant

Talkin Village, Hare & Hounds

Troutbeck, Mortal Man

Ullswater, Leeming on Ullswater Restaurant

Ullswater, Old Church Hotel Restaurant

Ullswater, Rampsbeck Hotel Restaurant

Ullswater, Sharrow Bay Hotel Restaurant & Lounge

Wasdale Head, Greendale Gallery Restaurant

Wasdale Head, Wasdale Head Inn

Windermere, Langdale Chase Hotel Lounge

Windermere, Miller Howe Hotel Restaurant & Lounge

Witherslack, Old Vicarage Hotel Restaurant

YORKSHIRE DALES

Aysgarth Falls, Mill-Race
  Teashop
Barden, Howgill Lodge
Barden, Low House Farm
Bolton Abbey, Bolton Abbey
  Tea Cottage
Carthorpe, Fox & Hounds
Constable Burton, Wyvill
  Arms
Dent, Dent Crafts Centre
Harrogate, Bettys
Harrogate, Vani's Pizzeria
Hawes, Cockett's Hotel
Ilkley, Bettys
Kettlewell, Racehorses Hotel
Kildwick, Kildwick Hall,
  Candle Lite Room
Kirkby Fleetham, Kirkby
  Fleetham Hall Restaurant
Kirkby Stephen, King's
  Arms Hotel
Otley, Chatters Tea Shoppe
  (Apr–Oct)
Pateley Bridge, Willow (L)
Settle, Car & Kitchen
Sutton Howgrave, White
  Dog Inn
Wath-in-Nidderdale,
  Sportsman's Arms (L)

AFTERNOON TEAS

CUMBRIA & LAKES

Alston: Brownside Coach
  House
Ambleside: Rothay Manor
Boot: Brook House
  Restaurant
Bowness on Windermere:
  Laurel Cottage
Caldbeck: Swaledale Watch
Hawkshead: Minstrel's
  Gallery
Melmerby: Village Bakery
Ullswater: Sharrow Bay
  Hotel Lounge
Windermere: Langdale
  Chase Hotel Lounge

YORKSHIRE DALES

Aysgarth Falls: Mill-Race
  Teashop
Barden: Low House Farm
Bolton Abbey: Bolton Abbey
  Tea Cottage
Harrogate: Bettys
Harrogate: Chimes
Ilkley: Bettys
Otley: Chatters Tea Shoppe

A guide to local markets & specialist food shops

MARKETS

Markets offer a great variety on the food front — from the standard fare of fresh fruit and vegetables to small one-man stalls selling specialist cheeses or a day's baking. A newcomer to the marketplace is the wholefood stall, which now flourishes alongside the long-established produce. Fish is rather poorly represented, especially in the Lakes, whereas prime British vegetables (only a few exotics) show that Yorkshire people really know their onions. It's worth remembering that many markets here are predominantly summer venues, as after September the number of stalls is drastically reduced. So, winter is not the best browsing or buying time for markets, especially those in Sedbergh, Hawes and Cockermouth.

CUMBRIA & LAKES

Appleby
Held Fri in market hall,
Sat in main street

Built along a stretch of the river Eden and dominated by a picturesque castle, Appleby is a pretty, friendly town which is perhaps best known for its annual horse fair. Every June gypsies arrive from all over the country to do business, bringing their mobile homes and colourful horse-drawn caravans with them. The weekly street market is a lively affair that grows bigger and busier during the summer months. (Friday's covered market is smaller and quieter.) The Eden valley is a rich agricultural area and there's plenty of locally-grown produce available in season. The meat and fish vans offer specialities like ox tail and tripe, while Stevensons' stall-cum-shop stocks a fine array of flowers, fruit and vegetables. Christine Johnston's baking is one of the biggest attractions: her scones, sponges and tea breads sell like the proverbial hot cakes!

David W Jones

Appleby Market

Carlisle
Held Mon—Wed, Fri & Sat
in market hall

A great indoor market which combines good produce with a wonderful atmosphere. Housed in the sturdy market hall with attractive ironwork reaching up to the ceiling, the stalls provide plenty of variety to choose from. Ernie Reay offers excellent seasonal vegetables and, if you've time to chat, he's full of fascinating snippets of information about curly kale, Jerusalem artichokes, year-round spring greens and the various potato varieties. Look for his 'own grown' labels – the taste is well worth it. You'd be hard pushed not to be tempted by the Coffee Centre's 29 different coffees and 48 teas. The Eden Valley Wholefoods unit beside one of the entrances may be small but it's stacked with a vast array of wholefoods plus ingredients for Indian and Chinese cooking. There's a separate fish section just off the main hall plus plenty of butchers supplying yards of Cumberland sausage and numerous haggis—a reminder of the proximity of the Scottish border.

Cockermouth
Held Mon in Market Street

A friendly, fairly small market in this prosperous town which is best known as the birthplace of William Wordsworth. The market doesn't take long to explore, although you're likely to be waylaid by the garrulous stallholders. Beyond the flower-seller with his persuasive line of patter is Townslays' fish stall, well stocked with fresh produce from as far away as Aberdeen. Across the road Joseph Mathews, an ex tax office man who opted out to run a smallholding with his wife, sells a wide range of home-reared and home-made goods. Marmalade, jams, lemon curd and teabreads crowd his stall alongside boiling fowl, chickens, ducks and free-range eggs. Next door, The Coffee Man (in reality Joe Gammond) has 20 different coffees on offer as well as 30 teas – and Swaledale sweaters.

Kendal
Held Wed & Sat
in market place &
Stramongate, also Sat
in market hall

The outdoor market has a fair mix of the usual cheap and cheerful clothes, sweets and flowers but the best part is in the market hall on Saturday mornings. It's here that there are still traces of the original farming market with women selling bunches of herbs, baskets of fresh eggs, a few fowl or just the one goose. There's local honey, too, as well as jams, jellies, fudges and, from Farmer Atkinson, rows of plump,

Kendal, the market place

E A Bowness

naturally-fed chickens. The best stall here is the huge, long cheese counter which runs across the back wall of the hall. Peter and Louise Gott's superb display (including Long Chawson Stiltons, Sturminster Cheddars and goat's and sheep's milk cheeses) draws crowds of shoppers all day.

Peter Gott (Kendal) has one of the finest cheese stalls you could hope for

Fruit & veg stall, Kendal Market

Pot plants for sale on Kendal Market

Kirkby Lonsdale
Held Thurs in market place

A very pretty market set out in a picturesque square in this lovely old town. It's a small market but a few of the highlights should not be missed. Join the queue by 10am for the WI stall, which does a roaring trade until just 11. Cakes, preserves, pickles and home-grown fruit and vegetables disappear fast as do the plants, cuttings and seedlings. On the nearby Keogh family stall, there are herb jellies produced from home-grown herbs, also jams, honeys, lemon curd, fudge and toffee. There's just one fruit and vegetable stall and another selling fish, also a sweets trailer with a tempting display of 250 varieties—all the old favourites like gobstoppers, humbugs and aniseed balls. Sights worth detouring for are the Devil's Bridge on the edge of the town and, through the churchyard, Ruskin's View—a stunning outlook which Ruskin claimed presented the finest view in the world.

Margaret Armstrong

Ulverston
Held Thurs & Sat in
Market Street, New
Market Street, behind the
market hall & in the old
auction rooms

*Muriel Dixon selling her own eggs
on Ulverston Market*

The largest and best of the Cumbria markets, excelling in bread and fruit and vegetables. Ulverston is on the tourist route—it's the home town of Stan Laurel and the Laurel and Hardy Museum in King Street attracts a steady stream of American visitors—but the market is down to earth and practical. Just inside the main front doors of the hall the Waltons sell their fine breads, including an outstanding granary loaf. Just the other side of the doors Mr Blackledge's cheeses, cooked meats and sausages are all very good, too. There are excellent fruit and vegetable stalls among the clothes, hardware and antiques. Go out of the back door for more market stalls and don't miss the old auction rooms where you will find Stan Fagan's home-made saucepans. Along the cobbled Market Street, there is a mixture of stalls selling flowers, farm eggs, chickens, ducks, pigeons, rabbits and excellent cheeses and yoghurts. In the fruit and vegetable line, there's everything from nuts and soft fruits in season to enormous field mushrooms and bunches of fresh herbs. Thursday's market is slightly bigger.

YORKSHIRE DALES

Hawes
Held Tues in main street
& market hall

In winter a bitter wind drives down the main street of this dour Pennine town, deterring all but the hardiest stallholders from setting up shop. As spring approaches, the market swells to its full quota, tractors and trailers crowd the parking spaces and shoppers converge in a seething mass of green wellies and waxed jackets. This is real farming country and there are plenty of noisy sheepdogs about to remind you of that fact. Mr Morrison's cheese trailer has a good selection of English and Continental varieties, including 14 different blue cheeses, while Stevensons' fruit and vegetable stall presents a glorious display of fresh, top-quality produce. The fish van with its limited stock of frozen white fillets and obligatory kippers reflects local demand: Pennine farmers prefer meat any day. Inside the market hall the Dales Wholefoods stall offers a healthy spread of pulses, pastas, dried fruits and home-made preserves.

Leyburn
Held Fri in main street

A wide street of weathered yellow sandstone houses makes a picturesque location for one of the prettiest markets in the Yorkshire Dales. Leyburn is a prosperous farming town situated in the heart of Wensleydale and you'll only find first-rate produce here. There are excellent fruit and vegetable stalls and the fish trailer displays a good mixed catch brought fresh from Whitby. If you're looking for cheese, something is bound to take your fancy from the 120 different varieties offered by Mr Morrison. Hazel Wetherill sells just eggs—free-range, deep-litter, pul-lets', ducks', all sizes. There are plenty of household goods and clothes, from pots and pans to shoes, bags, tweeds, green wellies and waxed jackets. Dales Wholefoods are here, too, selling thistle honey among the pulses, nuts and grains. The smell of coffee from Middleham's stall is deliciously tempting and they also sell tea and accessories like caddies and pots.

Geoffrey N Wright

Fruit & veg stall, Leyburn Market

Richmond
Held Sat in market place
& market hall

An attractive little market centred at the top of a cobbled hill. Tiny side alleyways and narrow streets lead off the market place and make for some exciting exploratory walks. On the food side, the show is stolen by the two Carrick trailers—one fish and fowl, the other fruit and veg. Their beautiful display of herring, halibut, mussels and home-smoked bloaters alongside duck, pheasant and chicken brings even non-shoppers to a standstill. And next door there are more queues for their top-quality fruit and vegetables. A small range of exotic fruits can be found further up the hill, and there's a cheese stall that's worth investigating. The bread and cake stall hails from Leeds and offers a vast selection of bakes, from scones and crumpets to Eccles cakes and Battenburgs, all carefully wrapped in cellophane. The indoor market hall, a short step down the hill, sells jewellery, toys, frozen foods and vegetables and there's a gem of a stall offering Jacobs wool merchandise – big shawls, ties, hats and jumpers.

Margaret Armstrong

Ripon Market, Country Products wholefood stall

Richmond Market, Steven Carrick holding a fresh salmon

Ripon
Held Thurs
in market place

This is the biggest and best of the markets tried out in the Yorkshire Dales and Lake District and is certainly one with a great atmosphere. The market square is packed on Thursdays with shoppers jostling round the wide variety of stalls. Excellent-quality vegetables, fruit, fish, eggs, health foods and cheese are just a few of the goods on sale. There're also two bacon stalls offering thick 'steaks', gammon joints and smoked bacon, and another doing a roaring trade in boxes of Belgian chocolates. Don't miss Margaret Darwin's stall stacked with baking bounty: wholemeal bread, tea loaves, date crumble, chocolate or cherry sponge, plus lots of biscuits and Welsh griddle scones.

All this is complemented by the usual range of stalls featuring clothes, plants, jewellery, toys and rugs.

Sedbergh

Held Wed in town's main
car park

A thriving summer market here but still a fairly good range of foods in winter. Nuts & Things, as you'd expect, specialises in a whole range of nuts as well as dried fruits, grains, pulses and herbs. There's fresh fish, too, and a fruit and vegetable stall, much of which is locally grown. Wilf Dixon's stall boasts fresh duck and chicken along with game in season. He also sells yoghurt, cheese and butter. Although the car park serves as the main market place there is also a small pitch outside the church, where the old country farmers' market was held. Here the two longest established stalls—one selling fish, the other fruit, vegetables and flowers—ply their wares.

Skipton

Held Mon, Wed, Fri & Sat
in main street

A big, busy market with stalls lining the whole length of the High Street, manned by cheerful, helpful vendors. There's been a market in Skipton, the southern gateway to the Dales, since the 7th century when wool was the main commodity. Stalls now offer rather more variety—clothes, tools, bags, bedding and a good range of produce. Fridays and Saturdays are best for food. The jovial group of women who run Tate & Sons' long vegetable stall say their speciality is 'service with a smile'. They certainly don't go in for exotica but concentrate instead on good-quality British veg—nice firm cabbages and leeks, plus freshly-pulled, leafy-topped carrots, parsnips, turnips, beetroots. There's nothing exceptional on the cheese front but plenty of other excellent produce—fish, meat, eggs, also health foods and toffees.

Fruit & veg stall, Skipton Market

SPECIALIST FOOD SHOPS

With the predominance of chain stores in every high street and the mushrooming of modern shopping malls, it's heartening to find so many excellent specialist shops. They are tended by dedicated and knowledgeable staff, and the emphasis is firmly on producing a prime product rather than on easy trading. As you'd expect, a number of these shops are long-established, family-run businesses using original recipes and methods, but many are new concerns stimulating new interest. The traditions of real farmhouse cheeses, for example, are not only being upheld but are being developed and expanded.

CUMBRIA & LAKES

Kendal
Farrer's Tea &
Coffee Merchants
13 Stricklandgate, Cumbria
Kendal (0539) 31707
Proprietors: Nicholas & Jane
Woolley
Open Mon–Sat 9am–
5.30pm

A delightful tea and coffee specialist housed in what must be one of the few remaining original shops in Kendal. Farrer's dates back to 1819 and the present proprietors have continued to maintain both the style of the shop and the standard of its products. The first part you step into is the tea area where one whole wall houses a fantastic array of original black and gold tea bins and tins. Scoops and funnels are used in serving your choice—Lady Londonderry, Earl Grey and Assam to name but a few, as well as a Farrer blend specially made up for the area's soft water (called Lakeland Tea). A few steps up from this room and you're in the coffee area, dominated by an enormous 1840 coffee grinder. The shop prides itself on buying the green beans on the London market and then having them roasted in Kendal. The beans, some in sacks on the floor, are sorted into 20 different blends—including the most popular, Farrer's No 1. Downstairs, the cellars have been converted into a coffee lounge (page 90)—an ideal setting in which to try out some of the newer and more exotic blends. (Recipe page 92.)

Farrer's: one whole wall houses a fantastic array of tea in original black and gold bins

Right: Neil Boustead cutting up a slab of toffee

Penrith

The Toffee Shop

7 Brunswick Road, Cumbria

Penrith (0768) 62008

Proprietors: Neil & Diane Boustead

Open Mon–Fri 9.30am–5.30pm, Sat 9am–5pm

The air's heavy with the deliciously sweet, sticky smell of toffee as you push open the door of this small, family-run shop. The source of the aroma is the kitchen at the back, where fudges and toffees are prepared in old jam pans every day. Now run by Neil and Diane Boustead, the business was started 24 years ago by Diane's parents and it's their secret recipes that are used today. The small range consists of butter and treacle toffee, and fudge in plain, chocolate and mint flavours. The reputation of The Toffee Shop has travelled (without the aid of any advertising) far and wide. Produce is sold around the world and the client list even includes a few sweet-toothed royals.

Andrew Morris

Waberthwaite
Richard Woodall
Lane End, near Bootle,
Cumbria
Ravenglass (06577) 237
Open Mon–Fri 8.30am–
12.15pm & 1.15–5.30pm,
Sat 8.30am–12 noon

As the west Cumbria coastal-road traffic thunders through the undistinguished village of Waberthwaite, it's easy to miss the general store and post office. Which is a great shame because, besides selling stamps and the bags, the shop specialises in traditionally cured, home-produced ham and sausages. This family-run side of the business starts directly behind the shop on the pig farm owned by Joseph Woodall. His brother, Richard, buys enough carcases for the shop's needs and then sets about curing them, using much the same methods as his great-great-grandmother who started the business over 150 years ago. Cumberland Royal Ham (cured in ale, molasses, vinegar, salt and sugar, then hung for at least 3 months) and a Parma-style variety (to which a herb is added during curing) are just two of the results. Richard and his wife June also make an excellent Cumberland sausage using only meat and seasoning, with no added water or cereals. The majority of the produce is sold on the premises but some can be found in delicatessens and specialist shops around the country; it's also available by mail order.

YORKSHIRE DALES

Harrogate
The Cheeseboard
1 Commercial Street,
North Yorkshire
Harrogate (0423) 508837
Proprietors: Joan Chantler &
Brenda Crosby
Open Mon, Tues & Thurs–
Sat 9am–5.30pm, Wed
9am–1pm

A cheese lover's paradise, this specialist shop stands out from other cheese stores not just because of the huge variety but also because all the cheeses are in prime condition. Rather than keeping the cheeses in refrigerated cabinets (which means having to bring them out into warmer temperatures to cut and wrap them) the whole shop is kept at a cool 0°C/32°F and the cheeses displayed on marble slabs. Once a product has passed its best it is withdrawn from sale. This attention to detail typifies the owners' attitude to their first venture into retailing. There are over 100 dfferent types of cheese from several countries. British varieties—which are all farmhouse, not mass-produced—include Jersey Milk Swaledale (made only at one small dairy), a nutty Double Gloucester, Blue Wensleydale and an excellent Stilton from Long Chawson. The French selection includes unpasteurised Brie and Camembert and there are interesting Swiss, Italian and Dutch varieties.

courtesy of The Cheeseboard

Joan Chantler & Brenda Crosby, The Cheeseboard

Ripon
King's
Old Market Place,
North Yorkshire
Proprietor: Bettys Harrogate
Open Mon–Sat 8.30am–5pm

As you walk into King's, the delicious aroma is just as tantalising as the visual appearance of the place. This excellent bakery owned by Bettys of Harrogate still sticks to the traditions and style established by the three King sisters at the turn of the century. A lot of the baking is done on the premises and the range is truly comprehensive. Plaits, bloomers, baps, cottage loaves and cobs are just a few of the different breads produced each day, and they will supply shapes and sizes to suit individual customer needs. There are also croissants, tea cakes, sponges and tarts as well as a wickedly tempting Bismarck—a sweet dough stuffed with an almond and fruit filling and topped with icing and flaked almonds. Meringues, yule loaves (made all year), marzipan fruits and savoury pork and apple slices provide further choice, and the shop also stocks teas and coffee beans to accompany it all.

courtesy of King's

The packed window display at King's attracts passers-by

Skipton
J. Stanforth: The
Celebrated Pork Pie
Establishment
9 Mill Bridge,
North Yorkshire
Skipton (0756) 3477
Proprietors: D & E Jabb
Open Mon, Wed & Thurs
7am–5.30pm, Tues
7am–12.30pm, Fri
6am–5pm, Sat 6am–4pm

The celebrated pork pies!

The queue that forms outside Stanforth's most days is an indication of the popularity of this shop's pies and meat products. The business is run by David and Elaine Jabb, who take pride in the fact that their pork pies are still made from a recipe handed down by Elaine's grandmother, the shop's founder. Made purely of pork meat encased in a crisp pastry crust, these celebrated pies are baked in batches throughout the day and there's always a delicious smell of fresh baking wafting through the shop. Stanforth's also sell local meat (pork and beef), home-made sausages, black puddings and brawn. And they do a roaring trade in cold cuts from their huge home-baked hams and joints of roast pork.

27

Snacks and Tracks around the Lakes & Dales

LAKE DISTRICT One-day tour of the North-western Lakes

This tour is a circular route from Keswick, one of the major Lakeland tourist centres.

Distance: About 40 miles

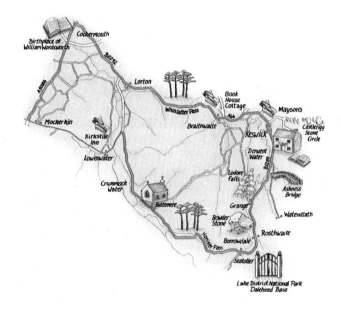

Keswick–Cockermouth–Keswick

O nce a thriving mining town, *Keswick* is now a mecca for fell walkers, climbers – and tourists. Shop for sheepskin, anoraks and Kendal mint cake; look round the Lakeland Craftsmen's Guild, the Cumberland Pencil Factory and museum or the town's own museum in Station Road, with its manuscripts and letters of the great Lakeland poets (Wordsworth, Coleridge and Southey), its well-documented geological exhibits, and musical stones. The Visitors' Information Centre is in the ancient Moot Hall in the market place (Saturday is market day).

Leave Keswick by the B5289, motoring towards Borrowdale. Take the left turn up to Watendlath over Ashness Bridge – a much-photographed beauty spot. Watendlath is a tiny hamlet in a fold of the fells with its own small tarn and rushing stream. Immortalised in The Herries Chronicles by novelist Hugh Walpole, it's well worth a short detour. Back on the B5289, drive alongside the lake, stopping at the Lodore Swiss Hotel to pay a token 5p or so to view the famous *Lodore Falls* – doubtless in full spate after recent rain!

Continue to Grange-in-Borrowdale, but don't miss the precariously balanced Bowder Stone (relic of the Ice Age) before driving through the picturesque Borrowdale valley to Rosthwaite, then Seatoller at the foot of Honister Pass. Visit the Dale Head base of the Lake District National Park, and then make the steep rise to the quarry-scarred summit of the pass. Pause to take in its stark grandeur before descending into the Buttermere valley, with its sweeping views of High Stile to the left.

Only a narrow neck of land separates Buttermere from Crummock Water (home of the char – a Lakeland fish speciality), and the road runs past the Scale Hill Hotel. Have coffee here, perhaps, to enjoy its 'historic' atmosphere, before making for Loweswater – and lunch at the **Kirkstile Inn** (page 98): a friendly welcome, beamed ceilings and good pub fare.

After lunch, follow the road along Loweswater, through Mockerkin, turning right on to the busy A5086 into *Cockermouth*. This bustling agricultural centre was the birthplace of William and Dorothy Wordsworth; the house, in the main street, belongs to the National Trust.

Leave Cockermouth by the B5292 and head for Lorton, taking a left fork just before the village itself, to climb over Whinlatter Pass through thickly wooded Forestry Commission land. Park at the Visitors' Centre and enjoy a woodland walk with – weather permitting – some spectacular views, before dropping down into Braithwaite to the cosy **Book Cottage** (page 67) for tea, spiced buns and a good browse.

Once through Braithwaite, you are soon back on the A66 and into Keswick. If it's fine, work up an appetite for dinner with a stroll up Castlerigg to the ancient Stone Circle (circa 1400 BC). Dinner at **Mayson's** in Lake Road (page 95), whose menu provides plenty of spicy interest, makes a satisfying end to the day.

Keswick lies between peak of Skiddaw & Derwent Water

LAKE DISTRICT Two-day tour from Coniston to Witherslack

This tour takes you through some of Lakeland's narrowest and steepest roads. It is not recommended for the ultra-nervous driver.

Day 1 distance: About 45 miles

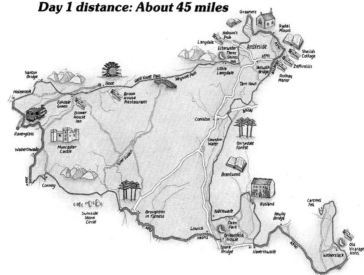

The South-western fells and coast to Little Langdale

Stay overnight at the comfortable **Bridgefield House**, just outside Sparkbridge (page 103), where David and Rosemary Glister will make you very welcome. After one of Rosemary's hearty breakfasts, drive through Sparkbridge to pick up the A5092. Turn towards Workington and drive through Lowick, with the lovely Coniston fells to the right and dramatic, quarry-scarred moorland to the left.

The road soon becomes the A595, skirting the sleepy village of Broughton-in-Furness and crossing the river Duddon. Take the minor road immediately to the right, following signs to Corney, driving first through a wooded valley, then rising on to open moorland on an unfenced road. Superb mountain vistas on the right vie with glimpses of the coastline on the left. (Look out for the footpath to Swinside Stone Circle, an ancient monument if you fancy a stroll.) Suddenly, as you reach the highest point, the ground rolls away, giving a breathtaking panorama of the western coast, the Irish Sea and – on a clear day – the Isle of Man.

Continue to Corney and the Ashdown Smokeries at Skellerah Farm, run by Harry Fellows. Here you can buy traditional, oak-smoked produce at the door. Leaving Corney, rejoin the A595, turning again towards Workington. Look out at Waberthwaite for the left turn to Richard Woodall's shop-cum-post office; behind it there's a thriving ham-curing business with its own pig farm (see Specialist Shops, page 24).

Next along the A595 there's *Muncaster Castle*, stately home of the Pennington family and famous for its rhododendron gardens. Visit the house (fine furniture and tapestries) or explore the grounds (nature trails) before driving on to Muncaster Mill for some stoneground flour to make the muffins on page 50. The mill is also a station for the *Ravenglass Railway*; once used for the iron mines and now a popular tourist attraction, the 15-inch gauge track runs almost seven miles up the Eskdale Valley to Dalegarth. There are trips daily from end-March to end-October.

Just as you enter Holmrook, take a sharp left on to a minor road signposted to Stanton Bridge and Eskdale Green for a climb through some wonderful mountain scenery (Scafell, Great Gable and Kirk Fell). At Eskdale Green, turn right for the **Bower House Inn** (page 78) and a substantial lunch in a friendly 'pub' atmosphere, or drive on to Boot to the **Brook House** (page 61), with its pizzas, omelettes and excellent pâtés.

Look at Boot's working water mill (now restored) and the pictures and crafts at Fold End Gallery before striking out over Hard Knott Pass. Dramatic views of the craggy mountain ranges compensate for the steep and narrow road, which needs the driver's full concentration! Drop down slowly, cross a packhorse bridge and make your way over the winding and appropriately named Wrynose Pass, driving first through barren mountains, then down into the greener pastures of the Langdale Valley. A right turn at an undefined junction brings you to Little Langdale and the **Three Shires Inn** (page 98), a charming pub where you can stay overnight.

For dinner, make the short drive through Skelwith Bridge to Ambleside for a wholefood pizza at **Zeffirellis** (page 57) or a more formal meal at **Rothay Manor** (page 55). Nearer 'home', there's **Hobson's Pub** (page 97) in the Pillar Hotel in Langdale.

Hard Knot Pass, dramatic views of craggy mountain ranges (left); Muncaster Castle, stately home of the Pennington family (right)

Day 2 distance: About 45 miles

Grasmere, Ambleside and Coniston Water

Leaving the Three Shires Inn, take the road to Elterwater, stopping perhaps at the weaving gallery, then bear left by the Britannia Inn, haunt of anglers and fell walkers. Follow signs to *Grasmere*, enjoying the views of lake and fells, then park and explore the village on foot. Note Sarah Nelson's (home of Grasmere gingerbread) and look round the church before finding Dove Cottage, Wordsworth's home from 1799 to 1808. There are shops, galleries and exhibitions as well as the 'museum' aspect to enjoy.

Take the A591 to *Ambleside*, passing Rydal Mount, Wordsworth's home from 1813 until his death in 1850 – and also open to the public. In Ambleside, make your way to **Sheila's Cottage** in The Slack (page 56, also recipe page 50) for lunch. This popular venue serves Swiss-style dishes (raclette cheese, Swiss chocolate cake and cream-topped drinks) as well as traditional Lakeland fare: char, Cumberland sausages and damson cobbler. If it's packed out, carry on down to the Garden Room Café in **Zeffirellis** (page 57). Good salads and quiches, and an excellent bakery if you prefer a picnic.

From Ambleside, take the A593 for *Coniston*, then turn left along the B5286 (Hawkshead) road, looking for the sign to the prettily situated Tarn Hows. Here you can park, admire the view and walk right round the tarn. From Tarn Hows, join the B5285, turning right for the head of Coniston Water. Take a left here and follow the minor road that runs down the east side of the lake on the edge of Grizedale Forest. Stop for a look round Brantwood, home of the 19th-century art critic and social reformer John Ruskin. Woodland walks, marvellous views over the water – and a bookshop – all add to the appeal.

Dove Cottage, Grasmere: home of Wordsworth 1799–1808

Right: Bridge House, Ambleside

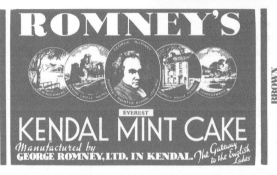

Drive on, along the lakeside, past Peel Island (featured in Arthur Ransome's children's adventure story Swallows and Amazons) and take the first left after Nibthwaite up a winding road to Oxen Park and Rusland. Here, at Georgian Hall, there's a well-known collection of self-playing musical instruments, some vintage photography equipment and a modern-day steam engine to inspect. Continue to Haverthwaite (don't miss the left turn just past Cobblestones restaurant), join the A590 and make for Newby Bridge. After the Lindale roundabout, turn left to Witherslack.

Another left turn in the village (Cartmel Fell) brings you to **The Old Vicarage** in Witherslack (page 116) for the night. This hotel is in a peaceful, woodland setting, yet within easy access of the busy main roads to Kendal, Barrow and Lancaster and the M6 motorway. All the dishes on the set menu (there's no choice) are prepared from prime local ingredients – superb vegetables, lovely sweets – and there's a well-chosen wine list (also see recipe, page 118). And if you're in no hurry to leave after breakfast, visit one of the two splendid stately homes nearby: Holker Hall near Flookburgh, or Levens Hall with its Elizabethan topiary gardens before heading home.

LAKE DISTRICT Two-day tour of the Northern Lakes, east to west
Day 1 distance: About 30 miles

Melmerby to Ullswater

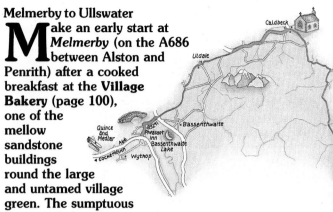

Make an early start at *Melmerby* (on the A686 between Alston and Penrith) after a cooked breakfast at the **Village Bakery** (page 100), one of the mellow sandstone buildings round the large and untamed village green. The sumptuous feast includes free-range eggs, home-baked breads, croissants and spiced buns straight from the ovens: avoid Mondays (they close except for Bank Holidays).

Leave by the A686 towards Penrith, turning right by the war memorial in Langwathby for Little Salkeld. Here you can visit the *Salkeld Water Mill*, where the flours used at the Village Bakery are still milled in the traditional way; buy your own to make their parkin (see recipe, page 92). After inspecting the mill, carry on up the hill to Long Meg and her Daughters, a Druid stone circle from which there are spectacular views of the northern Pennine range.

Return to the A686 and head for *Penrith*. Fishing enthusiasts will know of John Norris in Victoria Road and 'toffee-noses' will soon discover The Toffee Shop (see Specialist Shops, page 23). Don't miss the small Steam Museum up Castlegate.

Take the A6 southwards (signposted Shap and

Melmerby · Penrith   Cumbria CA10 1HE

Kendal), turn left at the signs for Cliburn and Bolton – and you're on your way to **Wetheriggs Pottery Centre** in the village of *Clifton Dykes*. This pink-washed complex of 19th-century buildings houses a small museum, a shop, a children's playground, a sculpture garden, a restaurant-cum-gallery and an ice cream parlour serving delicious Calthwaite ices. Run by Jonathan and Dorothy Snell (he's the potter, she's the weaver), Schofield's is a splendid place for lunch (page 74). Also see recipe page 50.

On leaving Wetheriggs, turn right, then right again

Melmerby

Long Meg and her Daughters

Little Salkeld

Village Bakery

Langwathby

Penrith

Mungrisdale

Clifton Dykes

Scofields

Abb

Wetheriggs Country Pottery

B5320

Askham Hall

Outbeck

Pooley Bridge

Askham

Melkinthorpe

Lowther

River Lowther

Matterdale

Aira Force

Watermillock

Dockray

Old Church Hotel

Ullswater

(signposted Melkinthorpe and Lowther) to reach the A6, and then follow signs to Lowther and Askham. The road takes you through the open parkland of the Lowther estate, past the castle ruins and the lovely church, then crosses the river Lowther (a sharp turn here) to reach *Askham*, a fine example of a linear village, with a wide main street, a beautiful church and Askham Hall (a Grade 1 listed building dating back to the 14th century), home of the Earl of Lonsdale. Turn right at the T-junction and at the edge of the village turn left to Celleron, travelling slowly along the narrow road and enjoying the pastureland scenery before gaining spectacular fell views over Saddleback (Blencathara) as the road joins the B5320 for Pooley Bridge.

Drive through *Pooley Bridge* at the head of Ullswater, with its dramatic backdrop of mountains and lake, then follow the A592 along the lakeside, through the hamlet of Watermillock, until you reach the **Old Church Hotel** on the left for your overnight stay (page 108). In a peaceful lakeside setting, with comfortable lounges and stylishly furnished bedrooms, it's the perfect place to relax. Dinner here is a set menu, changed daily, with Kevin Whitemore as head chef and his wife Maureen in charge of desserts.

Day 2 distance: About 33 miles

Ullswater to Bassenthwaite Lake

After a good breakfast and a leisurely stroll in the hotel gardens, set off along the A592 with the lake to your left, and you'll soon come to the National Trust car park at *Aira Force*. It's a short walk along a good path to the famous 60-foot falls, then back on the road for a lovely run along the A5091 to Dockray and Matterdale, with its old stone farm buildings. As you climb out of Matterdale, the landscape changes to bleak, open moorland with marvellous views of Saddleback (Blencathara) ahead.

Drive on through Troutbeck, turn left on to the A66, then take a right along the narrow, winding road signposted Mungrisdale and Caldbeck. Carry on, following signs to Caldbeck, and you are in the heart of John Peel country on the northern boundaries of the Lake District National Park – an open landscape with a character and charm all its own. *Caldbeck* itself (John Peel's village) is full of character.

Rising out of Caldbeck, the road passes through open grazing land, so keep the eyes 'peeled' for stray sheep and moorland ponies as you drive to Uldale. Go straight through the village, making for Bassenthwaite (and Keswick), and you are rewarded with more spectacular views of the fells. In Bassenthwaite village pick up the B5291 (signposted *Bassenthwaite Lake* and Cockermouth) and follow the signs for the **Pheasant Inn** (page 60), which is approached by a small slip road after you cross the A66.

This long, low inn with mellow-panelled lounges, big log fires and trimly kept bedrooms has great comfort and character. There are well-kept gardens in which to stroll; it's only a mile and a half from the village of Wythop, and vegetarians may like to make the short drive to Cockermouth for a meal at **The Quince and Medlar** (page 75). The inn itself is tucked away in a quiet backwater yet it is just a stone's throw from the busy A66 – for the next day's journey home.

YORKSHIRE DALES One-day tour of Nidderdale
Distance: About 40 miles

Ripon–Pateley Bridge–Ripon

As this day's tour is centred round *Ripon*, we suggest you stay overnight at the **Ripon Spa Hotel** (page 149). It maintains old-fashioned standards of service, and it's set in peaceful surround-

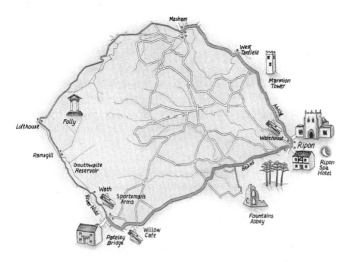

ings – next to a park yet handy for the town centre.

Before or after your drive, take a stroll round Ripon. There are many buildings of architectural interest, including the magnificent cathedral, with its 50-foot east window and rare Saxon crypt, and the 14th-century half-timbered Wakeman's House, now a small museum of local history. Among the many good shops you'll find several 'real' butchers (try Appleton's on the square for raised pork pies and cured hams), and enjoy the mouthwatering display at King's Bakery (see Specialist Shops, page 26). If you're feeling peckish, find the **Warehouse** (page 150), situated above a crafts shop, for coffee or a light lunch of wholemeal quiche, crisp salads – and delicious light cakes.

Turn left out of the Spa Hotel along the B6265 towards Pateley Bridge. Look for the signs to *Fountains Abbey* on the left and follow these along a lovely, secluded wooded valley to the splendid ruins of this Cistercian monastery, dating from 1132. Now owned by the National Trust, they are an impressive reminder of the simple grandeur of monastic life.

Back on the B6265, and still making for Pateley Bridge, the landscape changes from agricultural to moorland, with open views towards Grassington. Turn

Fountains Abbey, North Yorkshire

37

right at the T-junction about a mile before Pateley Bridge and leave the car (weather permitting) for a short stroll and some panoramic views of the surrounding countryside, before dropping down into the village. The river Nidd flows through *Pateley Bridge*, once a textile centre as well as a busy farming community, and there are pleasant riverside walks to enjoy as well as the Nidderdale museum to visit and learn about local history and folklore.

For lunch, there's the **Willow** (page 147) in Park Road for savoury éclairs or a wild rabbit pie; otherwise, drive on, cross the river and turn right along the narrow dales road leading to Wath-in-Nidderdale – and the **Sportsman's Arms** (page 153), a mellow, sandstone inn serving home-made soups, local trout or a generous ploughman's platter.

Continue, after your break, along the valley, past the Gouthwaite reservoir, through Ramsgill and along the riverside to Lofthouse. Here the road begins to climb over the heathery moors to Masham, giving marvellous views of the reservoir in the valley behind and tempting glimpses of the lush green valley and reservoirs ahead. There's a Regency folly to be seen on the right, just to add a dramatic point to the scene.

The road brings you down from the moors, through several pretty villages to Masham, where the great sheep fair is held each September. Take the A6108 back towards Ripon, looking out as you pass through West Tanfield for the Marmion Tower, a beautiful ancient monument of local honey-coloured sandstone.

YORKSHIRE DALES Three-day tour of the central Dales

This tour is a good mixture of open, bleak Dales country, gentle valleys, agricultural towns and lots of beautiful villages. Terrain and roads vary considerably.

Day 1 distance: About 54 miles

From Grassington to Skipton, and Settle to Hawes

The **Wilson Arms Hotel** in Threshfield (page 152), with its bright, spacious bedrooms and good ensuite bathrooms, makes an ideal starting point for this three-day tour of the Yorkshire Dales and fells. *Grassington* is just a short drive, so have a look round this popular Dales village, with its shops, galleries, cobblestoned centre and the Upper Wharfedale museum, before driving back past the hotel along the B6265 to *Skipton*.

It's likely to be a market day in Skipton, as there's one on Monday, Wednesday, Friday and Saturday (see Markets, page 21); the Castle is open to visitors and the museum in the Town Hall gives a clear picture of the local history, geology and archaeology.

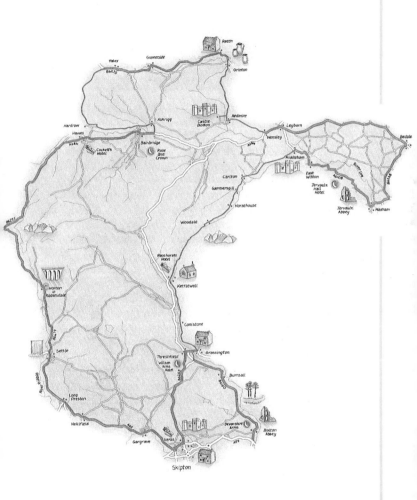

Before leaving Skipton, collect a picnic lunch: vegetables and fruit from shops or market stalls, pies from The Celebrated Pie Shop (see Specialist Shops, page 27) and something for dessert from Whitakers' Chocolate Shop in the High Street. Further along, there's an Aladdin's cave for wholefood-eaters at Healthilife. Have coffee in the upstairs café-restaurant (**Herbs Wholefood & Vegetarian Restaurant**, page 151 and recipe on page 118), and then set off along the A65 towards Settle. ▶

Ribblehead Viaduct (left); Skipton Castle, The Gateway (right)

The road takes you through a number of villages, with glimpses of the Leeds–Liverpool Canal to the left. *Settle*, a smaller community than Skipton, manages to retain its dignified, friendly air despite the intrusion of the busy A65 (there's a by-pass under construction), and there are some lovely buildings along the back streets. Tuesday is market day. Leaving Settle on the A65, turn right before crossing the river Ribble, and on to the B6479 for Horton in Ribblesdale. Have a quick look at the weir on your left – it's often an impressive sight!

The route takes you through a splendid limestone landscape, with its 'pavement' outcrops, caves and special flora. Once through Horton, there's a view of the splendid Ribblehead viaduct which carries the Settle to Carlisle railway – arguably the most scenic route in the country. The road joins the B6255 – turn right for Hawes through a rocky, barren territory dominated by the three famous Pennine peaks of Ingleborough, Whernside and Pen-y-Ghent, before dropping down from the open dales into the little town of *Hawes*.

Hawes has a good market on Tuesdays during the summer months (see Markets, page 18); there are country clothes shops (for tweeds, waterproofs, woollens and wellingtons) and an old-established grocer-cum-bakery (120 years) called Eliza Allen's, which sells individual truckles of Wensleydale cheese and its own rich fruit cake. At **Cockett's Hotel** (page 135) pause for some of Mrs Guest's shortbread, flapjacks, scones and home-made jam before leaving Hawes on the A684 for the peaceful village of Bainbridge – and the **Rose and Crown** (page 122).

This comfortable old coaching inn (see the Bainbridge horn) is at the end of the village green. It has a choice of bars, comfortably furnished bedrooms and is spotlessly kept – altogether a good place to relax at the end of the day.

Day 2 distance: about 54 miles

Askrigg through Swaledale and Wensleydale to
Jervaulx

Leave Bainbridge after a look at the river, village green and stocks, to drive the 1½ miles to Askrigg where Mrs Thwaite at Cringley Garth makes excellent Wensleydale farmhouse cheese from unpasteurised Jersey milk. Telephone first – (0969) 50504 – if you wish to call. Turn left in Askrigg and follow signs to Hardrow, turning right after about four miles on to the narrow fell road that rises to *Buttertubs*. Park at the top, where a notice gives details of the deep limestone holes which give this pass its name. Continue down and along Swaledale on the B6270 towards Richmond.

The road takes you through *Muker* (note the Swaledale Woollens Shop), past gently sweeping hillsides crisscrossed by limestone walls and dotted with lovely old stone barns, through to Reeth. Stop here and explore the craft workshops – pottery and knitwear – and the Swaledale Folk Museum. Continue along the B6270 and then in Grinton turn right for Redmire.

This road climbs steeply over bleak and open moorland before dropping into Wensleydale: look for the right turn to *Castle Bolton*, where the castle – one of the 'resting places' of Mary Queen of Scots and now a semi-ruin – is open to the public and has a museum. There should be good views from the castle over the Wensleydale valley.

Continue on to Redmire, a village that grew out of coal and lead mining; then turn left and follow signs to Leyburn, joining the A684 at Wensley.

Leyburn, with its wide main street and sturdy sandstone buildings, has the air of a thriving community, and market days (see Markets, page 19) are full of colour and bustle. The route along the A684 takes you through 'tamed' countryside with traditional, unspoilt, trimly kept villages and farms to Bedale, with its cobbled market place. You might visit the Bedale Bakery, owned by the same people as King's in Ripon (see Specialist Shops, page 26). Turn right just beyond, on to the B6268 for Masham, crossing the river Ure, and then fork right again along the A6108 for Middleham. Three-and-a-half miles further on, you come to the ruins of *Jervaulx Abbey* – a peaceful setting for the **Jervaulx Hall Hotel** (page 139) and an overnight stay. The hotel is in a handsome, 19th-century house with polished wood floors, fresh flowers, a spacious lounge and pretty pastel bedrooms. There's a croquet lawn for the energetic on long evenings.

Day 3 distance: About 35 miles

Jervaulx to Wharfedale, Wharfedale to Bolton Abbey

Take time for a walk after breakfast round the ruined abbey before leaving Jervaulx. Turn right out of the hotel drive back on to the A6108 in the direction of Middleham. Have a look round the picturesque village of East Witton before continuing to *Middleham*, in the heart of racehorse country. The town itself is set on a hill, and the history of its castle is connected with Richard III – around 1461. A network of narrow lanes and alleyways radiates from the market place, revealing old cottage dwellings behind the three-storey 'grandeur' of the market square.

Leave Middleham and make for Coverdale, rising on to open moorland, where you may be lucky enough to see some of the Middleham horses at the gallops. Take your time along this narrow, scenic route through trim, tidy villages – Carlton, Gammersgill, Horsehouse and Woodale – before descending down the steep slope into *Kettlewell*, with lovely views of Wharfedale ahead.

Kettlewell has an interesting jumble of buildings to explore, a lovely old church, the close proximity of the river Wharfe – and the 17th-century **Racehorses Hotel** (page 139) for lunch! There's a wide choice here, from simple bar snacks to steak pie, local trout, lasagne and a variety of cold meats and salads.

Suitably refreshed, take the lesser road out of Kettlewell down the left-hand side of the river – it's quieter and more scenic – to Conistone. The little road follows the Wharfe through a patchwork of lush, green fields bordered by limestone walls. From Conistone, pick up signs to Grassington, then take the Skipton road, bearing left as you cross the river to make for the B6160 and Burnsall, a very pretty village in a lovely setting by the river. From here it is not far to the famous – and popular – ruins of *Bolton Abbey*. Park and inspect them, taking one or more of the pleasant riverside walks before coming to rest at the **Devonshire Arms Hotel** (page 124), which faces the parklands of the abbey estates.

The hotel is both 'ancient and modern' and the styles blend well. Originally a fine coaching inn, it is now a spacious and delightful venue with two lounges, two bars (one lively, one quiet) and thoughtfully equipped bedrooms – each with its private bath or shower. It is conveniently set beside the A59 Harrogate to Skipton road for the journey home.

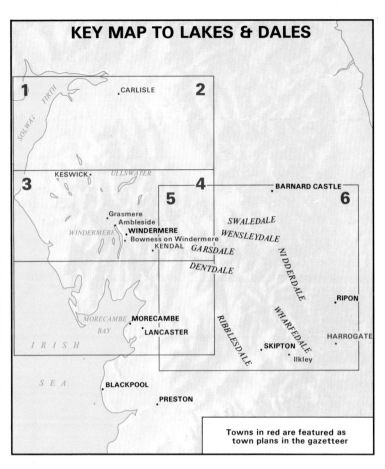

KEY MAP TO LAKES & DALES

1

SOLWAY FIRTH

CARLISLE

2

KESWICK

ULLSWATER

3

4

BARNARD CASTLE

5

6

Grasmere
Ambleside
WINDERMERE
Bowness on Windermere
WINDERMERE
KENDAL

SWALEDALE

WENSLEYDALE

GARSDALE

NIDDERDALE

DENTDALE

RIPON

MORECAMBE BAY

MORECAMBE

LANCASTER

RIBBLESDALE

WHARFEDALE

HARROGATE

IRISH

SEA

SKIPTON

Ilkley

BLACKPOOL

PRESTON

Towns in red are featured as
town plans in the gazetteer

LEGEND

▬▬▬ Motorway	▬▬▬ Primary route
▬▬⑩▬▬ Motorway with Junction number	▬▬▬ A road
▬▬Ⓢ▬▬ Motorway with Service area	═══ B road
▬▬▬ Dual Carriageway	═══ Unclassified road
Pateley Bridge Featured towns	▲ 3054 SKIDDAW Spot height

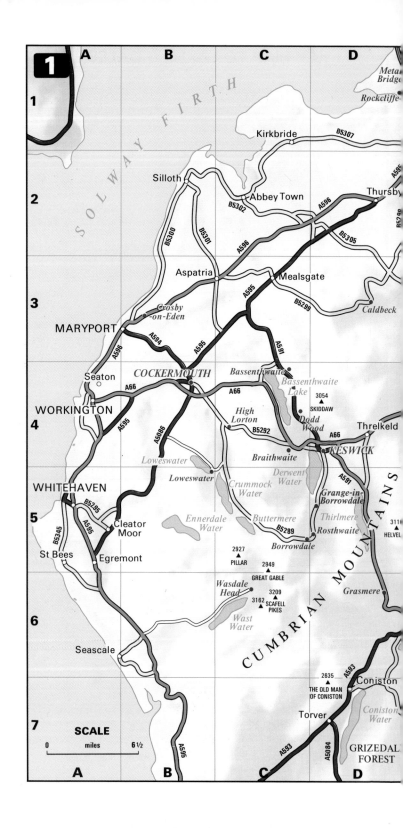

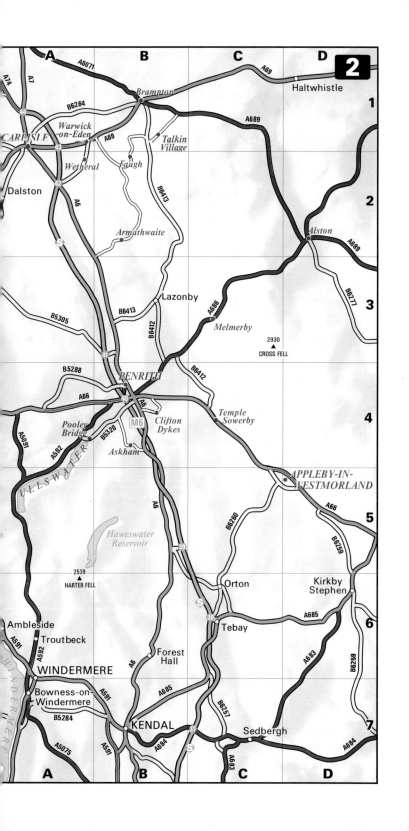

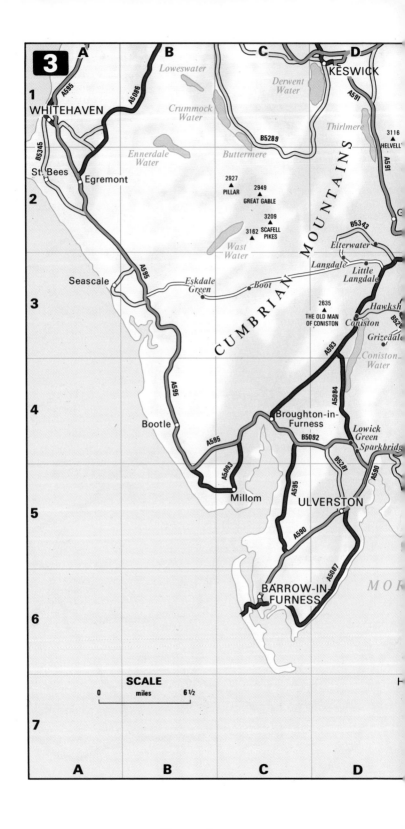

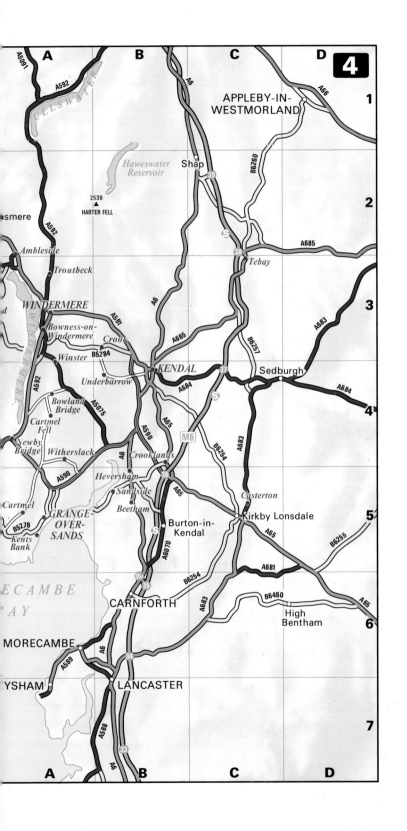

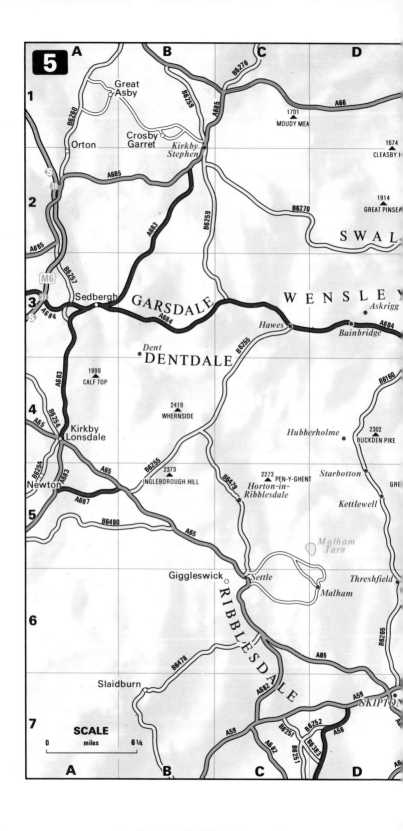

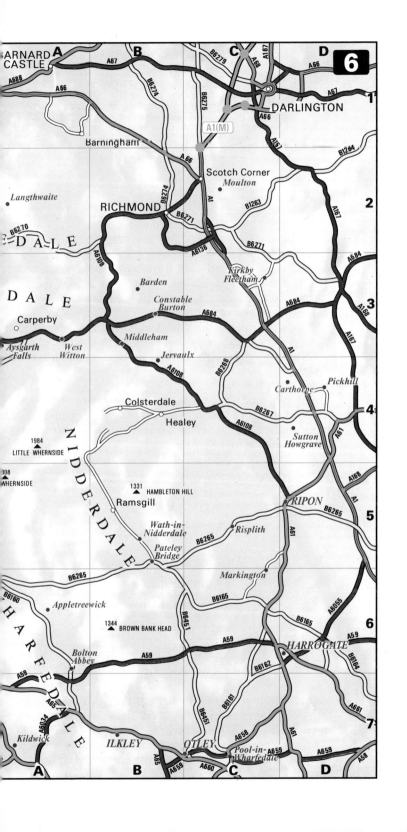

Sheila's Cottage
Ambleside
OLD ENGLISH MUFFINS

25g (1oz) sugar
75g (3oz) fresh yeast
1.4kg (3lbs) unbleached flour
15ml (1tbsp) salt
700–900ml (1¼–1½pts) warm water
a little cracked wheat

Dissolve the sugar in the water and crumble in the yeast. Allow to stand until frothing. Mix the flour and salt and add the liquid until you have a very moist, spongy dough. Knead well for 10–12 mins.

Set to prove in a warm, moist place for 1 hour or until well risen. Knock back the dough and cut into 125g (4oz) pieces, shape into small buns and top with a pinch of cracked wheat (be careful not to overwork the dough).

Place on a lightly greased tray and then gently roll a rolling pin over all the tops. Bake in a pre-heated oven at 220°C (425°F, Mark 7) for 10–15 minutes until the buns are nicely browned and sound hollow when tapped on the base. MAKES 16

Wetheriggs Pottery Centre, Schofield's
Clifton Dykes
BRAN MUFFINS

2 teacups bran
2 teacups wholewheat flour
2 teacups milk
1 teacup soft brown sugar
1 teacup mixed dried fruits
30ml (2tbsp) golden syrup or treacle
10ml (2tsp) bicarbonate of soda

Mix all the ingredients together thoroughly and spoon into deep paper cases, filling well. Bake in a pre-heated oven at 180°C (350°F, Mark 4) for about 10 minutes. Best kept in a tin for a few days as they become moister and stickier; can be served with or without butter. MAKES 12

CUMBRIA
AND THE
LAKE DISTRICT

Cumbria & The Lakes

Once a region of thriving wool, fishing and mining industries, constantly on the alert for attacks by Scottish raiders, the Lake District, comprising the larger part of Cumbria, now attracts raiders of a different sort since it contains some of the most beautiful and best-loved countryside in the British Isles. The variety of the landscape in this comparatively small area is astonishing. The lakes range from the 10½-mile length of sociable, busy Windermere to deserted tarns high in the fells, some hardly larger than the average living room but apparently bottomless and icy cold, even on the hottest midsummer day.

Should your tastes be more unconventional, Cumbria hosts the Gurning Championships at Eskdale, where contestants come from all over the world to frame their heads in a horse collar and pull the most hideous faces they can!

The melancholy beauty of the Lakes has always attracted writers and artists. The former homes of Beatrix Potter, William Wordsworth and John Ruskin are all open to the public at Sawrey, Grasmere and Cockermouth, and Coniston respectively.

Just a Bite

Alston	Brownside Coach House

Cumbria. Alston (0498) 81263.
Map 2D2 ● Open 10–6 ● Closed
Tues & October–Easter ● No
credit cards.

A neat little tea room in a converted coach house two miles outside Alston on the A686 to Penrith. Using good local ingredients – and her trusty Aga – Margery Graham offers lovely savoury snacks like bacon and egg pie, brisket of beef and smoked fish quiche salads, plus specials such as pork chops in barbecue sauce on weekends and in high season. Finish with delectable fresh strawberry or peach gâteau. Unlicensed. No dogs. *Typical prices* Smoked trout pâté with salad £2.80 Savoury minced beef pie served with jacket potato & peas £2.60 Afternoon tea £1.95. ● WC.

Ambleside
Ambleside's most notable feature is probably the tiny Bridge House built over Stock Ghyll. Formerly a summer house for Ambleside Hall, it is now a National Trust Information Centre. The centre of Ambleside is now, sensibly, a conservation area.

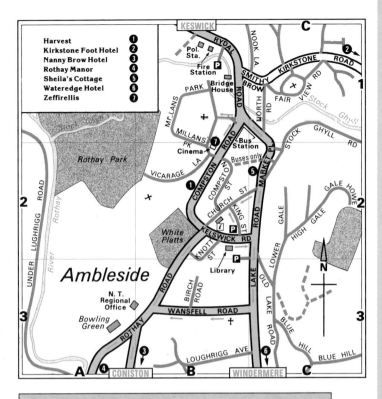

Harvest	❶
Kirkstone Foot Hotel	❷
Nanny Brow Hotel	❸
Rothay Manor	❹
Sheila's Cottage	❺
Wateredge Hotel	❻
Zeffirellis	❼

Ambleside   *Harvest*

Compston Road, Cumbria.
Ambleside (053 94) 33151 ● Town
plan B2 ● Open 10.30–2.30 &
5–8.30 ● Closed Thurs January–
June, also Mon–Wed January–
Easter & all November–
27 December ● No credit cards.

The food is well prepared, wholesome and full of flavour at
this attractive vegetarian restaurant whose outside is
brightened by troughs of flowers. Natural fruit juice,
marinated mushrooms or an excellent houmus could start
your meal, or maybe the day's soup (creamy bean and
vegetable when we dropped in). Quiche and various salads
are regular items on the menu, and each day brings two or
three hot specials such as vegetable pie – nice wholemeal
pastry – or Mexicali bean casserole. There's always a hot
crumble among the sweets, and all the cakes and biscuits are
made with 100% organic wholewheat flour. Children's menu.
Unlicensed. No smoking. *Typical prices:* Mexicali bean
casserole served with chopped raw salad £3.45 Banana,
honey and fruit split £1.25 Turkish honey cake £1.25. ◆ WC.

Hotel

Ambleside   *Kirkstone Foot Hotel*

Kirkstone Pass Road, Cumbria.	64%
Ambleside (053 94) 32232 ● Town	£D/E
plan C1 ● Bedrooms 14; En suite	
bath/shower 14; With phone 14;	
With TV 14 ● Confirm by	
arrangement ● Credit Access,	
Amex, Diners, Visa ●	
Closed 1–12 Dec & 22 Dec	
–13 Feb.	

Jane and Simon Bateman maintain high standards of
comfort and upkeep at this attractive white-painted hotel.
The relaxing lounge has a smart extension leading to a patio,
and there's a cosy bar. Prettily decorated bedrooms
(including three superior rooms with king-size beds) are
traditionally furnished; all have tea-makers, direct-dial
telephones and carpeted bathrooms. Half-board terms only.
Dogs in studio flats only. *Amenities* garden, croquet, laundry
service.

Restaurant

Ambleside
Kirkstone Foot Hotel Restaurant

Kirkstone Pass Road, Cumbria.
Ambleside (053 94) 32232 ● Town
plan C1 ● Lunch Sun only 12.30
for 1; Dinner at 8 ● Set L £6.50.
Set D £11.50. About £30 for two
● Credit Access, Amex, Diners,
Visa ● Closed 1–12 Dec
& 22 Dec–13 Feb.

Dinner is served promptly at 8 o'clock, after the gong has
reminded guests to take their places for Jane Bateman's five-
course dinners (no choice except desserts). Fillet of sole
dugléré might precede soup; then there is a hearty main
course – perhaps rack of lamb – followed by pudding and
cheese. No smoking until after sweets. Traditional Sunday
lunchtime roast. ☺

Hotel

Ambleside   *Nanny Brow Hotel*

Clappersgate, Cumbria. Ambleside	59%
(053 94) 32036 ● Town plan A3 ●	£E
Bedrooms 19; En suite bath/shower	
16; With phone No; With TV 19 ●	
Confirm by 6 ● Credit Access, Visa.	

About a mile west of Ambleside off the A593, this welcoming

hotel (once a private home) offers attractive accommodation, both in the garden wing, where the superior bedrooms and suites boast half-tester beds, and in the main house itself, where rooms are comfortably traditional. Most have spotlessly kept bath/shower rooms. Public areas include a lounge and intimate bar. Access to portable phone. *Amenities* garden, solarium, whirlpool bath, coarse fishing, water skiing.

Ambleside — Rothay Manor

71%
£C/D

Rothay Bridge, Cumbria. Ambleside
(053 94) 33605
● Town plan A3
● Bedrooms 18;
En suite bath/ shower 18; With

phone 18; With TV 18 ● Confirm by arrangement ● Credit Access, Amex, Diners, Visa ● Closed early Jan–mid Feb.

On the outskirts of Ambleside, this attractive Regency house has a warm, friendly atmosphere. Many fine features survive, notably a full-length verandah and a splendid doorway with the original glass. Comfortable furnishings, including some antiques, fill the lounge, where paintings and fresh flowers add a homely touch. Bedrooms, too, have the easy appeal of a private house, with bespoke pine furnishings and all manner of cosseting little extras, plus good modern bathrooms. One of the two handsome lodge suites is suitable for wheelchairs. No dogs. *Amenities* garden, croquet, laundry service.

Ambleside — Rothay Manor Restaurant

Rothay Bridge, Cumbria. Ambleside
(053 94) 33605 ● Town plan A3 ●
Lunch 12.30–2, Sun 12.30–1.30.
Dinner 8–9 ● Set L Sun only £8.50.
Set D £16.50. About £44 for two ●
Credit Access, Amex, Diners, Visa ●
Closed early Jan–mid Feb.

There's a delightful period feel about this comfortable restaurant, where the cooking is in the capable hands of Jane Binns. Set dinners could start with potted Stilton or prawns provençale, with soup before a main course like Breton lamb or tasty braised pheasant. Excellent English cheeseboard, and good puddings. Buffet lunches except for Sunday. No smoking. ☺ ♀ *WELL-CHOSEN* house wine.

Ambleside — Rothay Manor Lounge

★

Rothay Bridge, Cumbria.
Ambleside (053 94) 33605 ●
Town plan A3 ● Open 12.30–
2 & 3–5.30 ● Closed early
January–13 February
● Credit Access, Amex,
Diners, Visa.

The lounges with their antiques, paintings and fresh flowers
are pleasant places for a truly delicious snack, and the garden
is delightful in summer. Lunchtime brings soup, cold cuts,
salads and nice sweets, while teatime delights range from
scones with marvellous home-made jam to bara brith, spiced
apple cake and old-fashioned treacle tart. No dogs. *Typical
prices* Soup of the day 85p Set afternoon tea £3.50. ● ◎ WC.

Ambleside — Sheila's Cottage

★

The Slack, Cumbria.
Ambleside (053 94) 33079 ●
Town plan C2 ● Open 10.15–
5.30 ● Closed Sun, Bank
Holidays & January ● No
credit cards.

The Greaveses' marvellous cottage tea shop is renowned far
and wide for its simply splendid food. Kipper pâté flavoured
with dill and tomato, sugar-baked ham and potted shrimps
are typically tempting savouries, while sweet treats include
banana toffee flan and raspberry and hazelnut roulade.
Several interesting Swiss specialities, too. Lunchtime
minimum of £2.50. No dogs. *Typical prices* Vaudois savoury
£3.95 Cumbrian air-dried ham with pears £5. ● ◎ WC.

Ambleside — Wateredge Hotel

Borrans Road, Cumbria. Ambleside	60%
(053 94) 32332 ● Town plan C3	£D/E
● Bedrooms 20; En suite bath/	
shower 12; With phone No; With TV	
No ● Confirm by arrangement	
● Credit Access, Visa ● Closed	
December–January.	

A pleasant little hotel centring on a pair of fishermen's
cottages. The beamy bar is snug and inviting, and pleasant
lounges overlook the lawn that runs down to the lakeside

jetty. Bright, traditionally styled bedrooms are neat and shipshape, and the bathrooms have smart new suites and tiling. Half-board only. No children under seven. *Amenities* garden, coarse fishing, jetty, moorings, rowing boat, sailing boats, laundry service.

Ambleside   Zeffirellis

Compston Road, Cumbria.
Ambleside (053 94) 33845 ● Town
plan B1 ● Open Garden Room Café
10–5.30; Pizzeria 12–3 & 5–9.45 ●
Closed Tues & Wed November–
March except Christmas–January ●
Credit Access, Visa.

A stylish modern complex that includes a cinema. In the pizzeria, wheatmeal pizzas come in three sizes (plus a little one for children) with a variety of tasty vegetarian toppings. There's also fresh pasta, plus omelettes, ratatouille, cold plates and some good sweets. Excellent coffee and delicious home baking. No smoking. No dogs. *Typical prices* Pizza funghi £2.50 Lasagne with salad £3.85. WC.

Appleby   Royal Oak Inn

Bongate, Cumbria. Appleby (0930)   *(Food,*
51463 ● Map 2D5 ● Last bar food   *B & B)*
order 9 pm ● Bedrooms 7; With   £F
bath/shower 3; With TV 7 ●
Check-in: all day ● Credit
Access, Amex, Diners, Visa
● Closed eve 25 December
also accommodation 24 & 25
December ● Free House. Beers
McEwan's 70/–; Lager; Webster's
Yorkshire Bitter; Guinness; Beck's
Lager; cider.

The main bar of this long coaching inn is given old-world charm by oak beams, mellow panelling, brassware and antiques. Cooking here is honest and enjoyable, and the bar menu covers a fair span, from soup and pâté to langoustines with garlic butter, good-quality steaks and spicy bobotie. Boodles fool is a nice sweet. Children welcome. *Typical prices* Langoustines £3.95 Bobotie £2.95. ©

Bedrooms are of decent size, with tasteful colour schemes and reassuringly solid furnishings. All now have TVs and tea-makers, and nice home-from-home touches include a selection of good books. The bathrooms are well-equipped. Pleasant breakfasts.

Pub

Armathwaite — Duke's Head Hotel

Front Street, Near Carlisle, Cumbria. *(B & B)*
Armathwaite (069 92) 226 ● Map £F
2B2 ● Bedrooms 7; With bath/
shower No; With TV No ● Check-in:
all day ● No credit cards ● Closed
24, 26 & 31 December ● Brewery
Whitbread. Beers Whitbread Castle
Eden Bitter, Trophy, Best Mild;
Heineken; cider.

Excellent salmon and trout fishing draws anglers to this homely inn, which stands near an imposing stone bridge over the picturesque river Eden. Overnight accommodation is neat and simple, and the seven bedrooms, which all have washbasins and tea-makers, share two public bathrooms. The public and lounge bars are relaxing spots for a drink and a chat, and the hotel has an attractive walled garden. Children welcome.

Pub

Askham — Punch Bowl

Penrith, Cumbria. Hackthorpe *(Food,*
(093 12) 443 ● Map 2B4 ● Last bar *B & B)*
food order 9.30 pm ● Bedrooms 5; £F
With bath/shower 1; With TV No ●
Check-in: restricted ● Credit
Access ● Closed eve 25 December
● Brewery Whitbread. Beers
Whitbread Castle Eden Ale, Trophy,
Mild; Guinness; Heineken; Stella
Artois; cider.

The M6 is only 10 minutes away, but this 17th-century sporting inn enjoys a peaceful setting in a delightfully unspoilt village. The bar has lots of character, with beams and a log-burning stove, and it's a great favourite locally. Bar food spans an imaginative range, from subtly spiced curried apple soup and houmus with pitta bread to chicken Kiev, Chinese-style spare ribs and the very tasty minced beef cobbler with its dumpling-type crust. Sandwiches, salads and well-kept English cheeses are available for lighter bites, and there are some nice puddings such as peach meringue or lemon ice-cream cake. Children welcome. *Typical prices* Spare ribs £2.95 Pâté £1.50. ☺

The five bedrooms, all decent-sized doubles or twins, are simply but tidily furnished; housekeeping is good, and there's always plenty of hot water for the washbasins. Tea-making facilities are provided. Patio.

Pub

Askham · Queen's Head Inn

Near Penrith, Cumbria.	(B & B)
Hackthorpe (093 12) 225 ●	£E/F
Map 2B4 ● Bedrooms 5; With bath/	
shower No; With TV No ● Check-in:	
all day ● No credit cards ● Brewery	
Vaux. Beers Ward's Bitter; Vaux	
Sunderland Bitter, Mild; Lorimer's	
Scotch; Guinness; Tuborg: cider.	

Dating back to 1682, this fine cottage inn is kept in tip-top condition by the caring Askews. Fresh flowers and pretty ornaments lend a homely air to the comfortable lounge and beamed main bar, a delightfully welcoming room with its gleaming oak furniture and open fire. Bright, appealing bedrooms share two equally well-kept bathrooms. Children welcome but no under sevens accommodated overnight. No dogs in rooms. Patio. In the grounds is a model railway to delight young and old alike.

Hotel

Bassenthwaite · Armathwaite Hall

Near Keswick, Cumbria.	66%
Bassenthwaite Lake (059 681) 551	£D
● Map 1C4 ● Bedrooms 39; En suite	
bath/shower 39; With phone 39;	
With TV 39 ● Confirm by 4 ●	
Credit Access, Amex, Diners, Visa.	

The setting for this handsome 17th-century mansion is quite superb – 133 acres of park and woodland bordering lovely Bassenthwaite Lake. The hotel has a lake frontage extending 1½ miles, and the views are really glorious. The entrance hall has a wealth of mellow panelling and lots of trophies, and there's an elegant lounge and a cosy bar with an ornately carved mantel. A stylish leisure centre with its own bar has been created from the old coach house. Good-sized bedrooms are furnished in traditional or more modern style, and all have trouser presses and hairdryers. Bathrooms vary somewhat, from smart, roomy ones with bidets and pretty tiling to others rather more ordinary – but still perfectly OK – and seven with just showers. *Amenities* garden, sauna, indoor swimming pool, solarium, whirlpool bath, gymnasium, tennis, squash, coarse fishing, snooker, pool table, table tennis, 24-hour lounge service, laundry service (Mon–Fri), valeting.

Our inspectors never book in the name of Egon Ronay's Guides; they disclose their identity only after paying their bills.

Pub

Bassenthwaite Lake   Pheasant Inn

Near Cockermouth, Cumbria.	*(Food,*
Bassenthwaite Lake (059 681) 234	*B & B)*
● Map 1C4 ● Last bar food order	£D
2 pm, Sun 1.30 pm ● Bedrooms 20;	
With bath/shower 20; With TV No ●	
Check-in: all day ● No credit cards	
● Closed 25 December ● Free	
House. Beers Theakston's Best	
Bitter; Bass; Guinness; Carlsberg	
Hof.	

Picture a typical old English inn – long and low with a rustic porch, whitewashed walls and mossy slate roof. The Pheasant fits the bill perfectly and is only a few minutes walk away from picturesque Bassenthwaite Lake. Inside, at lunchtime, you can order a pleasant snack in the charmingly old-fashioned bar that's hung with hunting prints. There are potted shrimps, smoked salmon, game pâté, soup, smoked trout or eel, Cumberland pork, ham and egg pie and cold meat platter, to name a few. Avocado vinaigrette and cottage cheese and pineapple salad provide choice for vegetarians. Breakfasts are carefully cooked and served with strong hot tea, and there's also a restaurant. No children in the bar on Sundays. *Typical prices* Sweet smoked chicken £2.20 Ploughman's lunch £1.70 (No bar food eves). ☺

Bedrooms are excellent. Each one is furnished differently but they are all crisp, clean and light, and one has a half-tester bed. All have good, well-equipped private bathrooms. Service is excellent: beds are turned down, shoes cleaned and early morning tea served in rooms. No dogs in rooms.

Pub

Beetham   Wheatsheaf Hotel

Near Milnthorpe, Cumbria.	*(B & B)*
Milnthorpe (044 82) 2123 ●	£F
Map 4B5 ● Bedrooms 8; With bath/	
shower 2; With TV 7 ● Check-in: all	
day ● No credit cards ● Free	
House. Beers Thwaites Bitter;	
Younger'sBitter; Stones Bitter; Bass	
Mild; Guinness; Carlsberg; cider.	

The Miller family's pub has long been a popular stopping off place for travellers on the A6. There's a choice of three bars, two cosily traditional in character, plus a panelled upstairs lounge with TV. Seven neatly furnished bedrooms all offer TVs and tea-makers; two have private facilities, the rest share two neat simple public bathrooms. Children welcome.

Boot — Brook House Restaurant

Holmrook, Eskdale, Cumbria.
Eskdale (094 03) 288 ● Map 3C3 ●
Open 8.30 am–8.30 pm ● Closed
November–Easter ● No credit
cards.

A large, creeper-clad house in beautiful Eskdale is the setting for some splendid home cooking and baking. Breakfast goes on until mid-morning, after which there's a really extensive choice, from sandwiches, pâtés and omelettes to oven-baked trout, Cumberland sausage and steak and mushroom pie for the hungriest walker. Set teas offer anything from scones to a fry-up, and puds include meringues, fruit pies and delicious-looking cakes. *Typical prices* Cumberland sausage £2.45 Houmus £1.80. ● ☺

Boot — Woolpack Inn

Eskdale, Holmrook, Cumbria.	*(B & B)*
Eskdale (094 03) 230 ● Map 3C3 ●	£F
Bedrooms 7; With bath/shower 4;	
With TV No ● Check-in: all day ●	
Credit Visa ● Free House.	
Beers Younger's Scotch, IPA;	
Carlsberg; Harp; cider.	

This friendly inn nestling in the Eskdale Valley is just the place to recover from the tortuous gradients of the Hardknott Pass. Thirsty hikers tend to annexe the main bar, but the lounge with its open fire is very cosy, and there's a chintzy residents' lounge. Delightfully old-fashioned bedrooms have tea-makers and electric blankets. Four have shower cubicles; the rest share a spotless bathroom. Children welcome. Garden.

Borrowdale

Considered by many to be the most beautiful valley in the Lakes, it is indubitably the wettest in England with a rainfall of over 130″ per year at its head (the Lodore Falls are spectacular after heavy rain). A side road branching off at Ashness leads to Watendlath, supposed home of Hugh Walpole's fictional heroine Judith Paris. A charming, remote hamlet, it is best explored on foot so as to enjoy the stunning view across Derwentwater and Bassenthwaite. Beyond the 'Jaws of Borrowdale', where the valley narrows dramatically, is the remarkable Bowder Stone which is 2000 tons in bulk and perched on its smallest point.

Borrowdale   Borrowdale Hotel

Near Keswick, Cumbria.	60%
Borrowdale (059 684) 224 ●	£D/E
Map 1C5 ● Bedrooms 35; En suite	
bath/shower 35; With phone 35; With	
TV 35 ● Confirm by 4 ● Credit	
Access, Visa.	

This handsome greystone hotel overlooking Derwentwater is itself overlooked by towering peaks. There's a relaxing lounge decorated with pictures of local scenes and a modern bar which uses light oak to good effect. Neat bedrooms, some with antiques, others more contemporary, have remote-control TVs, hairdryers and smart bathrooms. Guests have free use of a nearby golf course. Half-board terms only. *Amenities* garden, laundry service.

Borrowdale   Lodore Swiss Hotel

77%
£ C/D

Near Keswick, Cumbria.
Borrowdale (059 684) 285 ●
Map 1C5 ● Bedrooms 72; En
suite bath/shower 72; With
phone 72; With TV 72 ●
Confirm by arrangement ●
Credit Amex ● Closed 2 Nov–
26 March.

A family hotel par excellence, with extensive grounds offering lovely views over Derwentwater, superb staff and an almost endless list of things to do. Doing nothing is a pleasure, too, as the immaculate public rooms are particularly comfortable and relaxing. Bedrooms are stylishly appointed, with a host of extras (and 24-hour room service to boot!). Well-equipped bathrooms. Run by the England family for 40 years. No dogs. *Amenities* garden, indoor & outdoor swimming pools, solarium, keep-fit equipment, sauna, tennis, squash, dancing (Sat), 24-hour lounge service, beauty salon, in-house movies, children's playground & nursery, games room, laundry room & laundry service, kiosk.

Our inspectors never book in the name of Egon Ronay's Guides; they disclose their identity only after paying their bills.

Borrowdale
Lodore Swiss Hotel Restaurant

Near Keswick, Cumbria.	
Borrowdale (059 684) 285 ●	
Map 1C5 ● Lunch 12.30–2. Dinner	
7.30–9.30 ● Set D from £14.	
About £34 for two ● Credit Amex ●	
Closed 2 November–26 March.	

The kitchen brigade does a consistently fine job and the restaurant staff work with almost unmatched efficiency and precision. Fixed-price menus offer terrines and mousses, fresh fish, high-quality meats, interesting vegetables and sensational pâtisserie. Finish with a selection from the notable cheeseboard. Excellent wines at reasonable prices. ℮

Borrowdale
Lodore Swiss Hotel Lounge

★

Near Keswick, Cumbria.	
Borrowdale (059 684) 285 ●	
Map 1C5 ● Open 10–7 ● Closed	
2 Nov–mid Mar ● Credit Amex.	

Lovely panoramic views accompany impeccably served sweet or savoury snacks. Swiss dishes like restbrot (cold meat open sandwich) or a ploughman's with three types of Swiss cheese, grapes and salad make elegant light lunches, but the high spot must be the heavenly pâtisserie – including chocolate sachertorte and fresh strawberry cheesecake. No dogs. *Typical prices* Spinach & mushroom salad with garlic croûtons £2 Set afternoon tea £3.90. ◆℮ WC.

Bowland Bridge   *Hare & Hounds*

Grange-over-Sands, Cumbria.	*(B & B)*
Crosthwaite (044 88) 333 ● Map	£F
4A4 ● Bedrooms 9; With bath/	
shower 4; With TV 9; ● Check-in: all	
day ● No credit cards ● Free	
House. Beers Tetley's Bitter, Mild;	
Guinness; Skol; cider.	

Dating back to 1600, this fine old inn enjoys a peaceful valley setting. The spacious, softly lit main bar makes an atmospheric spot for a quiet drink, and prettily decorated bedrooms in the original building also have considerable appeal. They share two modern bathrooms, while remaining rooms – located above the pool room bar – have en suite showers. Children welcome. Garden.

Bowness

Bowness was originally the port for Windermere Lake, its name deriving from Bull's Nose (meaning promontory), when the main industry of the area at that time was char fishing. Ferries have plied across the lake from Bowness since 1454; in the churchyard of St Martin's is a common grave for 47 souls who were lost when the ferry capsized in 1635.

Bowness on Windermere Belsfield Hotel

Kendal Road, Cumbria. Windermere	62% £C/D
(096 62) 2448 ● Town plan B2 ●	
Bedrooms 66; En suite bath/shower	
66; With phone 66; With TV 66 ●	
Confirm by 6 ● Credit Access,	
Diners, Visa.	

Good leisure facilities and an attractive position overlooking Lake Windermere make this handsome Victorian house a popular holiday hotel. Comfortable public areas include a spacious lounge, library and modern bar. Smartly fitted bedrooms all have good tiled bathrooms. *Amenities* garden, sauna, indoor swimming pool, solarium, tennis, dancing (Sat), 24-hour lounge service, children's playground, putting, games room, table tennis, pool table.

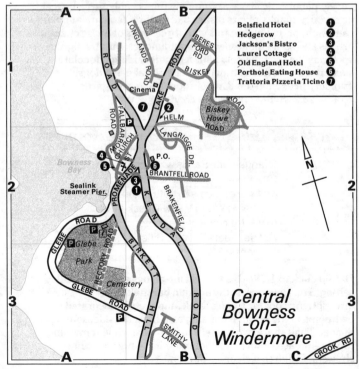

Belsfield Hotel ❶
Hedgerow ❷
Jackson's Bistro ❸
Laurel Cottage ❹
Old England Hotel ❺
Porthole Eating House ❻
Trattoria Pizzeria Ticino ❼

Central Bowness -on- Windermere

Bowness on Windermere   Hedgerow

Greenbank, Lake Road, Cumbria.
Windermere (096 62) 5002 ●
Town plan B1 ● Open 11–9 ●
Closed Tues & Wed October–April
& 2 weeks November ● Credit
Access, Diners, Visa.

A cheerful, pine-furnished restaurant serving wholesome and imaginative vegetarian fare. Starters include tempting pâtés – avocado with cottage cheese and Brazil nut – which could be followed by a salad, chilli or cheese bake. Finish with a seasonal fruit crumble or perhaps raspberry Pavlova. Cakes and scones available all day. No smoking. *Typical prices* Avocado pâté with salad £1.50 Lasagne with salad £3.40. ● WC.

Bowness on Windermere
Jackson's Bistro

West End, Cumbria. Windermere
(096 62) 6264 ● Town plan B2 ●
Dinner only 6–10, from 7 in winter ●
About £27 for two ● Credit Access,
Amex, Visa ● Closed Mon, 3 weeks
January & 25 & 26 December.

The menu changes roughly every two months at this friendly, extremely popular cellar bistro with a splendid old kitchen range. Typical dishes produced by Frank Jackson include seafood pancakes, lamb casserole with pickled red cabbage and baby halibut with prawn and mushroom sauce. Cooking is wholesome and enjoyable, and there are some delightful homely sweets like hot fruit charlotte to finish. ☺

Bowness on Windermere Laurel Cottage

St Martin's Square, Cumbria.
Windermere (096 62) 5594 ● Town
plan A2 ● Open 2.30–5.30 July–mid
September, also Bank Holidays & 1
week Easter ● Closed Sat ● No
credit cards.

A lesson in good eating goes on at teatime in this former school house, under Cathy and Paul Jewsbury's tutelage. Sandwiches, excellent egg mayonnaise, scones, home-made cakes and a truly memorable sponge studded with walnuts add up to an enjoyable spread, not to mention tempting banana loaf and teacakes. Unlicensed. No dogs. *Typical prices* Open prawn sandwich £2 Cream tea £1.40. ● WC.

Hotel

Bowness on Windermere
Old England Hotel

Church Street, Cumbria.	65%
Windermere (096 62) 2444 ● Town	£C
plan A2 ● Bedrooms 82; En suite	
bath/shower 82; With phone 82;	
With TV 82 ● Confirm by 6 ●	
Credit Access, Amex, Diners, Visa.	

A converted Victorian house by Lake Windermere. Antiques and period pieces fill the public rooms, which include a large lounge and two bars. Best bedrooms are the 26 in a modern block with attractive furniture and good tiled bathrooms; refurbishment will bring main-house rooms to the same standard. Parking is limited. *Amenities* garden, outdoor swimming pool, solarium, golf practice net, mooring, health & beauty salon, hairdressing, snooker, laundry service.

Restaurant

Bowness on Windermere
Porthole Eating House

3 Ash Street, Cumbria. Windermere
(096 62) 2793 ● Town plan B2 ●
Dinner only 6.30–10.30, Sat 6.30–
11 ● About £36 for two ● Credit
Access, Amex, Diners, Visa ●
Closed Tues & mid December–mid
February.

Honest, flavoursome cooking and a real desire to satisfy the customer have built up a loyal following at this family-run Italian restaurant. The standard menu (minestrone, excellent spaghetti, veal escalopes, steaks) is supplemented by interesting specials like fish consommé, poached turbot and penne alla zingara. Lovely liqueur-laced puds. ☺
▣ *OUTSTANDING* ♀ *WELL-CHOSEN* house wine

Just a Bite

Bowness on Windermere
Trattoria Pizzeria Ticino

53 Quarry Rigg, Lake Road,
Cumbria. Windermere (096 62) 5786
● Town plan B1 ● Open 10–2 & 6–
10.30; 10–3 & 6–11 in summer ●
Closed Thurs, 1 January & 25 & 26
December ● No credit cards.

Pizzas and pasta dishes are favourite choices at this attractive Italian restaurant with a few outside tables. Pizzas range from basic tomato sauce, mozzarella and oregano to the della casa with a little bit of everything. Pasta lovers can try rigatoni with ratatouille or spaghetti with seafood, or stick with tried and tested varieties like bolognese or carbonara. There's a special light lunchtime menu and a more elaborate choice on the evening menu. No dogs. *Typical prices* Scaloppine all' Bellinzona £3.95 Frutti di mare alla Sophia £4.25. WC.

Braithwaite   Book Cottage

Near Keswick, Cumbria. Braithwaite (059 682) 275 ● Map 1C4 ● Open 10–12.30 & 2–5.30 ● Closed Thurs & November–Easter ● No credit cards.

Mary Walsh runs this simple – even spartan – little tea room that's in a converted barn, and in the same building you'll find her brother's second-hand book shop featuring over 6,000 volumes for sale. Her list is rather more limited – traditional scones and spice buns served with jam and cream, delicious ginger cake, lovely rich date and orange slice, oat biscuits and sandwiches, all to be enjoyed with a good cuppa. Everything is carefully prepared and entirely recommendable. There's a pretty garden. Unlicensed. No smoking. *Typical prices* Ginger cake 50p Scone with cream & jam 55p. ●.

Braithwaite   Ivy House Hotel

Near Keswick, Cumbria. Braithwaite (059 682) 338 ● Map 1C4 ●	60% £F
Bedrooms 8; En suite bath/shower 8; With phone No; With TV 8 ● Confirm by arrangement ● Credit Access, Diners, Visa ● Closed 21 November–6 March.	

The heart of this welcoming hotel in a small lakeland village is the beamed lounge furnished with winged armchairs and warmed by twin log fires. Drinks are served here and there's plenty of comfortable seating, too, in the handsome entrance hall. Most of the roomy bedrooms are appointed mainly in traditional style (two have four-posters) and all offer tea-makers, hairdryers and electric blankets. Good bathrooms. All in all, a peaceful place usefully situated for walkers. No children under 12. No dogs.

Hotel

Brampton — Farlam Hall Hotel

72%
£C/D

Hallbankgate, Cumbria.	
Hallbankgate (069 76) 234 ●	
Map 2B1 ●	
Bedrooms 13;	
En suite bath/ shower 13;	

With phone No; With TV 13 ● Confirm by arrangement ●
Credit Access, Amex, Diners, Visa ● Closed Mon & Tues in
Dec & Jan, all Feb, 1st 2 weeks Nov & 1 week Christmas.

A farmhouse in the 17th century, later enlarged to form a
major house, Farlam Hall is now a most delightful country
house hotel. The setting is superb – beautiful gardens with a
stream and ornamental lake – and guests could not wish for
friendlier hosts than the Quinion family. The decor is
splendidly traditional in the public rooms, which include a
homely entrance hall and comfortable lounges with antiques,
fine paintings and rich fabrics. Most of the bedrooms have a
sitting area, and all offer books, magazines and mineral
water. Well-equipped bathrooms are modern except for one
with Victorian mahogany fittings. Inclusive terms only. No
children under five. *Amenities* garden, croquet.

Restaurant

Brampton
Farlam Hall Hotel Restaurant

Hallbankgate, Cumbria.
Hallbankgate (069 76) 234 ● Map
2B1 ● Dinner only 7.30 for 8 ● Set D
£14, Sat £14.50. About £35 for two●
Credit Access, Amex, Visa ● Closed
Mon & Tues in December &
January, all February, 1st 2 weeks
November & 1 week Christmas.

Guests are asked to arrive at 7.30 and order in the cosy bar or
front lounge. The meal is served by friendly, charming
waitresses in an elegant dining room: three courses, plus
cheese and coffee, consisting of enjoyable dishes like delicate
watercress quenelles, seafood pancakes and tastily sauced
saddle of hare with green noodles. Simple sweets like toffee
and banana pie from the sideboard. ℮

Brampton   Tarn End

Talkin Tarn, Cumbria. Brampton
(069 77) 2340 ● Map 2B1 ● Lunch
12.30–1.45. Dinner 7.30–9 ● Set L
£10. Set D £15.50. About £44 for
two ● Credit Access, Amex, Diners,
Visa ● Closed D Sun in winter
& all February

Although the chef is Italian, the menu is firmly French at this
pleasant restaurant with rooms, which stands all on its own at
the end of a lake. Strips of lamb, sautéed in hazelnut oil and
served warm on a bed of mixed lettuce, makes a delightful
starter, and main dishes could include trout stuffed with
capers, olives and mushrooms, roast wild duck and fillet of
pork with ginger and brown sugar sauce. Vegetarian dishes,
too. To finish, perhaps crêpes Suzette or a whisky-zipped
chocolate mousse. Must book for set lunch (otherwise à la
carte). ☺

Bedrooms 6; With bath/shower 4.   £E

Six attractively decorated bedrooms with TVs and tea-makers
provide pleasant overnight accommodation. Bathrooms,
some with shower only, are smartly tiled, clean and neat. No
dogs.

Caldbeck   Swaledale Watch

Whelpo, Near Wigton, Cumbria.
Caldbeck (069 98) 409 ● Map 1D3
● Open 2.30–6 ● Closed Mon
(except Bank Holidays) & October–
end of May ● No credit cards.

In the tiny hamlet of Whelpo, this delightful farmhouse tea
room is well worth a visit for Nan Savage's splendid home
baking. Cider, nut and honey cake and rich fruit scones are
two of the favourite treats, and there are also lovely fruit pies,
buttery buns, quiche and baps with the filling of the day.
Unlicensed. No smoking. No dogs. *Typical prices* Cider, nut
& honey cake 32p Cream tea £1.20. ☙ WC.

Changes in data may occur in establishments after the Guide
goes to press. Prices should be taken as indications rather
than firm quotes.

Hotel

Carlisle

Now the county town of Cumbria, Carlisle was founded in AD 80 by Agricola. Luguvalium, as it then was, flourished during the Roman period. After the departure of the Romans it fell successively to the Picts, Vikings and Scots. The Normans reclaimed it for England in 1092 and began the building of the castle, continued by King David of Scotland and then by Henry VIII. The impressive twelfth-century Norman keep and the fourteenth-century main gate survive to this day. The castle once housed Mary Queen of Scots as a prisoner.

Carlisle   Crest Hotel

Kingstown, Cumbria. Carlisle (0228) 31201 ● Town plan B1 ● Bedrooms 98 ● En suite bath/shower 98; With Phone 98; With TV 98 ● Confirm by 6 ● Credit Access, Amex, Diners, Visa.	57% £C/D

A low-rise hotel next to junction 44 of the M6. Open-plan public rooms have been attractively upgraded, with soft pinks and pale greys creating a restful, well-coordinated look. There's ample writing space in the bright, functional bedrooms, which have tea-makers and trouser presses, plus neatly fitted bathrooms. *Amenities* garden.

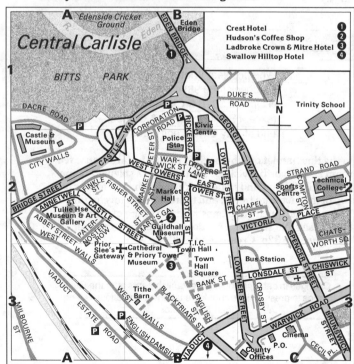

Central Carlisle

Crest Hotel	❶
Hudson's Coffee Shop	❷
Ladbroke Crown & Mitre Hotel	❸
Swallow Hilltop Hotel	❹

Carlisle — Hudson's Coffee Shop

Treasury Court, Fisher Street,
Cumbria. Carlisle (0228) 47733 ●
Town plan B2 ● Open 9.30–5
(Thurs till 4) ● Closed Sunday &
Bank Holidays ● No credit cards.

Friendly waitress service ferries cakes and snacks between the pretty dining room and flowery courtyard of this delightful little coffee shop. A light scone, caramel shortbread or delicious chocolate slice goes well with a pot of tea or a cup of coffee. Sandwiches are also available all day, and at lunchtime there are salads, variously filled jacket potatoes and specials like steak and kidney pie. No smoking. No dogs. *Typical prices* Quiche with 4 Salads £2.45 Ploughman's lunch £1.50. ⊜ WC.

Carlisle — Ladbroke Crown & Mitre Hotel

English Street, Cumbria. Carlisle	56%
(0228) 25491 ● Town plan B3 ●	£D
Bedrooms 98; En suite bath/shower	
98; With phone 98; With TV 98 ●	
Confirm by 6 ● Credit Access,	
Amex, Diners, Visa.	

The lofty entrance hall proclaims the Edwardian origins of this city-centre hotel, the scene of some welcome improvements. Public areas include two bars, one with a railway theme. Best of the bedrooms have been refurbished (new carpets, new light fittings, matching fabrics); others are more functionally equipped. *Amenities* indoor swimming pool, keep-fit equipment, in-house movies.

Carlisle — Swallow Hilltop Hotel

London Road, Cumbria. Carlisle	56%
(0228) 29255 ● Town plan B3 ●	£D
Bedrooms 110; En suite bath/	
shower 97; With phone 110; With	
TV 110 ●Confirm by 6 ● Credit	
Access, Amex, Diners, Visa.	

Good leisure and conference facilities exist at this modern hotel by the A6. Accommodation is of a fairly modest nature, ranging from attractively redecorated rooms to a few more basic ones without private facilities. *Amenities* sauna, indoor swimming pool, whirlpool bath, solarium, keep-fit equipment, dinner dance (Sat), coffee shop (11 am–7 pm), in-house movies, discothèque, pool table, laundry service.

Cartmel

Cartmel is best known for its priory, which dates from
1188, although only the gatehouse and the church remain.
The church was restored in the seventeenth century and is
now the parish church. The gatehouse, which stands in
the village square, was used as a grammar school from
1624 to 1790; it is currently an art gallery and folk museum
owned by the National Trust.

Hotel

Cartmel	Aynsome Manor Hotel

Near Grange-over-Sands,	60%
Cumbria. Cartmel (044 854) 276	£E
● Map 4A5 ● Bedrooms 15;	
En suite bath/shower 13;	
With phone No; With TV 15 ●	
Confirm by arrangement ●	
Credit Access, Amex, Visa ●	
Closed 1st 3 weeks January.	

Well-tended grounds and unspoilt countryside provide a
lovely, tranquil setting for this welcoming old manor house.
It's also within sight of the famous old priory. The entrance
hall doubles as a cosy lounge, with antiques, fine porcelain
and comfortable fireside chairs. There's a splendid first-floor
lounge – reached by a handsome cantilevered staircase – and
a little rustic bar. Smartly appointed bedrooms include two in
converted stables; simple carpeted bathrooms. Half-board
terms only. *Amenities* garden.

Just a Bite

Cartmel	St Mary's Lodge

Near Grange-over-Sands, Cumbria.
Cartmel (044 854) 379 ● Map 4A5 ●
Open 2.30–5 ● Closed mid
November–end March ● No credit
cards.

A friendly welcome and some delicious home baking await
visitors to this neatly kept little guest house standing near the
priory in picturesque Cartmel. Mrs Gaskins provides lovely
lemon and chocolate cakes, cream sponges, scones and
several sorts of loaves, including date and walnut, pineapple
and moist banana. Home-made jams are another treat, and
raspberry Pavlova provides further temptation. Unlicensed.
No smoking. No dogs. *Typical prices* Set afternoon tea
£2.05 Pavlova 60p. WC.

Cartmel · Uplands

Haggs Lane, Cumbria. Cartmel (044 854) 248 ● Map 4A5 ● Lunch 12.30 for 1. Dinner 7.30 for 8 ● Set L £8. Set D £14, About £38 for two ● Credit Access, Amex ● Closed L Mon & all early January–mid February

Tom (the chef) and Diana Peter run this pleasantly situated Edwardian house in partnership with Miller Howe's John Tovey. The menus feature the finest raw materials, sympathetically handled to produce excellent dishes like pea, pear and watercress soup, carefully marinated loin of lamb and poached fillet of plaice stuffed with smoked salmon and mango. Nice wholemeal bread and good sweets like lemon and lime cheesecake and rhubarb crumble. Smoking discouraged. ☺

♀ *WELL-CHOSEN* house wine.

Bedrooms 4; With bath/shower 4	£E

For diners only there are four pleasant bedrooms with TVs and simple white furnishings. No children under 12.

Cartmel Fell · Mason's Arms

(Food)

Strawberry Bank, Near Grange-over-Sands, Cumbria. Crosthwaite (044 88) 486 ● Map 4A5 ● Last bar food order 8.45 pm ● No credit cards ● Closed 25 December ● Free House. Beers McEwan's 70/–, 80/–; Wadsworth's 6X; Guinness; Kronenbourg; Beck's Bier; cider.

The excellent bar food and range of specialist and guest beers draw an appreciative crowd to this fine old converted farmhouse. In the beamed bars or at the table on the terrace you can enjoy an exotic collection of dishes, from tandoori chicken and stuffed vine leaves to gravlax and hearty coachman's casserole – beef in red wine with tomatoes, shallots, chestnuts and mushrooms. Salads and sandwiches provide lighter bites, and there are vegetarian specials and some truly memorable desserts. Children welcome. *Typical prices:* Chinese-style chicken wings £1.95 Nut roast en croûte £3.25. ☺

Our inspectors never book in the name of Egon Ronay's Guides; they disclose their identity only after paying their bills.

Casterton   Pheasant Inn

Near Kirkby Lonsdale, Cumbria.	(B & B)
Kirkby Lonsdale (0468) 71230 ●	£E/F
Map 4C5 ● Bedrooms 10; With bath/	
shower 10; With TV 10 ● Check-in:	
all day ● No credit cards ● Free	
House. Beers Thwaites Traditional	
Mild; Younger's Scotch Bitter;	
Tuborg; Beck's Lager; cider.	

All is commendably neat and tidy at this nice-looking
pebbledash pub, which has a pleasant little patio as a
summer alternative to the beamed bar. Four of the ten
bedrooms are traditionally furnished (one has a four-poster),
while the rest use decent white fitted units. There are TVs and
tea-makers in every room, and en suite bathrooms are smart
and modern. One room on the ground floor has been specially
fitted out for disabled guests. Residents have their own
comfortable lounge. Children welcome.

Clifton Dykes
Wetheriggs Pottery Centre, Schofield's

Near Penrith, Cumbria. Penrith
(0768) 62946 ● Map 2B4 ● Open
10–5, also Fri & Sat 7–9 pm ●
Closed 25 December ● Credit
Access, Visa.

Part of a complex that includes weaving and pottery
workshops, a museum and a sculpture garden. The restaurant
has a cosy homely feel, the food is good, and people very
friendly. Bran muffins, chocolate gâteaux and flapjacks are
popular quick snacks, with cauliflower cheese, deep quiches
and honey-baked ham among the more substantial items.
Fresh fruit salad, super ice cream, fine teas and coffees.
Sunday brunch. Set meals Fri & Sat eve £8. *Typical prices*
Leek & potato soup with roll 95p   Filled jacket potato &
salad £1.50. ℮ WC.

Cockermouth
A solid, historic old town, Cockermouth was given its
market charter in 1221 and by the seventeenth century
was the chief commercial centre of Cumberland. Its main
claim to fame is as the birthplace of Fletcher Christian,
Bounty mutineer, and William Wordsworth.

Cockermouth   Quince & Medlar

★

13 Castlegate, Cumbria.
Cockermouth (0900) 823579 ●
Map 1B4 ● Open 7 pm–9.30 pm
(Fri & Sat till 10) ● Closed Sun,
Mon & Bank Holidays ● Credit
Access, Visa.

Next to Cockermouth Castle, this well-run vegetarian
restaurant offers wholesome, high-quality eating in a quiet,
candlelit setting. The mouthwatering menus change monthly:
typical dishes include apple and peanut soup, baked
courgettes with rosemary and a Parmesan crumble top,
curried mixed vegetables and a super seed and nut bake with
tomato and celery or Stilton and mushroom sauce. End
memorably with a marvellous lemon cheesecake. No
smoking. *Typical prices* Seed & nut bake £4.60 Spinach &
cream cheese nut crumble £3.80. ● ⊜ WC.

Cockermouth   Wythop Mill

Embleton, Cumbria. Bassenthwaite
Lake (059 681) 394 ● Map 1B4 ●
Open 10.30–5.30, also Thurs 6.30–
8.30; Nov–Jan Sat & Sun 10.30–
4.30, also Fri & Sat 6.30–8.30 ●
Closed Mon, also end Oct–Easter
(except weekends Nov–Jan) ● No
credit cards.

A mother and daughter team are responsible for the excellent
home cooking at this gleaming tea room in a converted
sawmill. Their super scones and cakes are delicious with tea
or coffee, and at lunchtime you can tuck into cheesy baked
potatoes, pasta, soups and savoury flans, with lovely nutty
crumble to finish. Bookings only for the evening. Minimum
lunchtime charge £2. No smoking. No dogs. *Typical prices*
Vegetable lasagne with garlic bread £2.80 Blackcurrant &
apple nutty crumble with cream 85p. WC.

Coniston
Coniston is famous as the site of the waterspeed records
set by Donald Campbell in his 'Bluebird' powerboats. After
he died in 1967 in a further effort to raise the record,
permission was given for world record attempts to
continue on the lake to honour his memory. Also to be
found here is Brantwood, former home of John Ruskin.

Coniston	Bridge House Café

Cumbria. Coniston (0966) 41278 ●
Map 3D3 ● Open 10–5 ● Closed
end October–March except
weekends in February ● No credit
cards.

The pavement and the courtyard are pleasant for snacking in
the sun, and inside it's cheerful and cottage. Mrs Durston
produces an abundance of good baking, including spicy fruit
cake, flapjacks, banana bread and king-size gâteaux. Toasted
snacks, quiche and ravioli feature among the savoury choice,
along with salads, bumper sandwiches and a daily special
such as hot pot with red cabbage. No dogs. *Typical prices*
Ham sandwich & salad garnish £1.10 Fruit cake 50p. WC.

Coniston	Coniston Sun Hotel

Cumbria. Coniston (0966) 41248 ●
Map 3D3 ● Bedrooms 11; En suite
bath/shower 11; With phone No; With
TV 11 ● Confirm by arrangement ●
Credit Access, Visa ● Closed
January & February.

61%
£E

Standing at the edge of the village at the foot of Coniston Old
Man, this smartly painted old inn is ably run by a mother and
daughter team. Plants, flowers and books lend a homely air to
comfortable public rooms like the bright lounge with French
windows opening on to the garden. Prettily decorated
bedrooms, many enjoying fine views, offer tea-makers and
excellent modern bathrooms. *Amenities* garden.

Crook	Wild Boar Hotel

Near Windermere, Cumbria.
Windermere (096 62) 5225 ● Map
4B3 ● Bedrooms 38; En suite bath/
shower 38; With phone 38; With TV 38
● Confirm by arrangement ●
Credit Access, Amex, Diners, Visa.

63%
£C/D

This cordial country hotel stands among hills and woodland
on the B5284, west of Crook. There's a warm traditional feel
about day rooms like the Cockpit Bar and spacious lounge
with its well-upholstered armchairs and settees. Neatly kept
bedrooms offer a wealth of extras, from fresh fruit and
miniature sherries to hairdryers and remote-control TVs.
Amenities garden, dinner dance (Sat October–Easter).

Crooklands *Crooklands Hotel*

Near Milnthorpe, Cumbria. Crooklands (044 87) 432 ● Map 4B4 ● Bedrooms 15; En suite bath/shower 15; With phone 15; With TV 15 ● Confirm by 6 ● Credit Access, Amex, Diners, Visa.	60% £D

Attractive accommodation and a convenient position close to junction 36 of the M6 make this former coaching inn a useful overnight stop. Tastefully appointed bedrooms with fitted units have tea-makers, fruit and thoughtfully equipped bathrooms. The cosy bars have considerable rustic appeal. *Amenities* game & coarse fishing, laundry service.

Crosby-on-Eden *Crosby Lodge Hotel*

Near Carlisle, Cumbria. Crosby-on-Eden (022 873) 618 ● Map 1B3 ● Bedrooms 11; En suite bath/shower 11; With phone No; With TV 11 ● Confirm by arrangement ● Credit Amex, Diners, Visa ● Closed 24 December–late January.	66% £D/E

Looking from the distance very much like a castle, this handsome Georgian mansion boasts attractive gardens and lovely country views. Fine antiques distinguish the entrance hall, and there's a cheerful bar and inviting lounge. Bedrooms, both simple and grand (two have splendid half-testers), are spotless. Bathrooms range from well equipped to sumptuous. *Amenities* garden, laundry service.

Crosby-on-Eden *Crosby Lodge Hotel Restaurant*

Near Carlisle, Cumbria. Crosby-on-Eden (022 873) 618 ● Map 1B3 ● Lunch 12–1.45, Sun 12–1.30. Dinner 7.30–9 ● Set L £9.75. Set D £14.50. About £38 for two ● Credit Amex, Diners, Visa ● Closed D Sun to non-residents & 24 December–late January.

Michael Sedgwick's fixed-price menus are the thing to go for at this charming restaurant. Fresh ingredients are treated with flair and respect, and diners appreciate the generous helpings and imaginative fare. Subtle sauces transform traditional roasts, fish and steaks, while the sweet trolley is irresistible. ☺ ♀ *WELL-CHOSEN* house wine.

Just a Bite

Dodd Wood   Old Sawmill

Underskiddaw, Near Keswick,	
Cumbria. Keswick (0596) 74317 ●	
Map 1C4 ● Open 10.30–5.30 ●	
Closed end October–2 weeks	
before Easter ● No credit cards.	

The food may be simple, but what they do they do very well at this tea room, a former sawmill with views of Bassenthwaite Lake. Woodman's lunch – Cheddar and Cheshire cheese with French bread and pickles – is a popular order, and there are good sandwiches (plain or toasted), soup and salads. On the sweet half of the menu are home-baked scones, cakes and apple pie. Unlicensed. No smoking. No dogs. *Typical prices* Cumberland ham salad £2.70 Toasted sandwiches £1. ⊖

Pub

Elterwater   Britannia Inn

Near Ambleside, Cumbria. Langdale	*(B & B)*
(096 67) 210 ● Map 3D2 ●	£E/F
Bedrooms 10; With bath/shower No;	
With TV No ● Check-in: all day ●	
Credit Access, Visa ● Free House.	
Beers Hartley's XB Bitter; Tetley's	
Bitter; Bass, Bass Special;	
Guinness; Skol; Carling Black	
Label; cider.	

Overlooking the green of a picture-book village at the entrance to the Langdale Valley, this white-painted pub is a popular haunt of locals and walkers alike. The cosy little beamed bar with its attractive Lakeland stone fireplace is often packed, but residents can take refuge in the chintzy, book-stocked lounge. Simple, cheerful bedrooms with tea-makers share two well-kept bathrooms. TV is available in the rooms on request. Children welcome. Terrace.

Pub

Eskdale Green   Bower House Inn

Holmbrook, Cumbria. Eskdale	*(Food,*
(094 03) 244 ● Map 3B3 ● Last bar	*B & B)*
food order 9 pm ● Bedrooms 21;	£F
With bath/shower 15; With TV 15 ●	
Check-in: all day ● No credit cards	
● Closed accommodation only 3	
days Christmas ● Free House.	
Beers Hartley's Best Bitter;	
McEwans; Scotch Bitter; Guinness;	
Carlsberg; Foster's; cider.	

The friendly Smith family make everyone feel thoroughly at home in this charming slate-roofed inn. The setting, among the peace and beauty of Eskdale, is really delightful, and the beamed bar is warm and inviting. Bar snacks are fresh and appetising: soup, salads and sandwiches are always available or for something more substantial you could start with smoked mackerel pâté and go on to rabbit cooked in ginger ale or succulent poussin with a lemon sauce. Apple crumble is a popular pud, and there are some good English cheeses. Children welcome. *Typical prices* Steak & kidney crock pie £2.75 Venison in red wine £3.25. ☺

Bedrooms are of two types: six simply and traditionally furnished in the main house and 15 in a converted stable annexe that offer a higher standard of comfort: modern furnishings, colour TVs and good bathrooms. There's a comfortable, chintzy residents' lounge and a pleasant garden.

Faugh — String of Horses

Pub

Heads Hook, Near Carlisle, Cumbria. Hayton (022 870) 297 ● Map 2B2 ● Last bar food order 10.15 pm ● Bedrooms 13; With bath/shower 13; With TV 13 ● Check-in: all day ● Credit Access, Amex, Diners, Visa ● Closed accommodation only 3 days Christmas ● Free House. Beers Theakston's Best Bitter; Younger's Scotch Bitter; Murphy's Irish Stout; Webster's Yorkshire Bitter; Carlsberg Hof; Foster's.

(Food, B & B) £D/E

Oak beams, open fires and antiques contribute to the fine period feel of this 17th-century hostelry set in a quiet village. In the lounge bar a good choice of soundly prepared food is served: lunchtime brings an extensive cold buffet (Mon to Fri), plus grills, curries and specials like tasty beef goulash. In the evenings, seafood and salads are popular orders, along with dishes like lamb cutlets or Cumberland sausage. Sandwiches are available both sessions, and sweets include a very good chocolate gâteau. There's also a restaurant. Children welcome. *Typical prices* Beef goulash £3.25 Chicken suprême with lemon butter sauce £3.75. ☺

The bedrooms, including three four-poster suites, are individually decorated and furnished in luxurious, flamboyant style; cosseting extras abound, and the ornate bathrooms would not look out of place in Hollywood.

Grange-in-Borrowdale
Grange Bridge Cottage

Keswick, Cumbria. Keswick (0596)
84201 ● Map 1D5 ● Open 10.–5.30
● Closed Mon (except Bank
Holidays & July–September), also
November–Easter except
occasional weekends ● No credit
cards.

Next to a stone bridge across the Derwent, this charming,
cottagy tea room is a popular spot with summer visitors. A
fine dresser displays a tempting assortment of scones and
cakes – rich fruit, lemon and orange – which you can enjoy at
any time of day. Savoury alternatives range from home-made
soup to pizzas, houmus and the daily hot special such as
pasta bake. Unlicensed. No smoking. No dogs. *Typical prices*
Ploughman's lunch £1.75 Cottage pie with salad £1.75. ⊝

Grange-over-Sands   At Home

Danum House, Main Street,
Cumbria. Grange-over-Sands
(044 84) 4400 ● Map 4A5 ● Open
10–2 ● Closed Sun, Mon,
25 December–1 January, February
& November ● Credit Access.

Very much a family business, with Howard Johns the genial
host and his wife Jean and their daughter in the kitchen.
Morning coffee gives way at noon to soup, salads, omelettes
and open sandwiches, plus daily specials like smoked
mackerel pâté or a very good chicken and ham pie. Nice
puds, too, such as chocolate fudge cake or a toothsome
gooseberry and strawberry pie – an unusual combination that
works well. More elaborate evening menu. *Typical prices*
Asparagus & ham quiche £2.60 Italian trifle £1.05. ⊝

Grasmere
Although Wordsworth is associated with other places in
the Lake District, notably Cockermouth, Rydal and
Hawkshead, Grasmere is probably his best-known base.
Dove Cottage, where he lived with his sister Dorothy and
entertained the literary luminaries of the day, is now a
delightfully preserved little house, open to the public.
Wordsworth, his wife Mary, and some of their children are
buried in the churchyard of St Oswald's. In addition, the
village is renowned for, and well stocked with, the famous
Grasmere gingerbread.

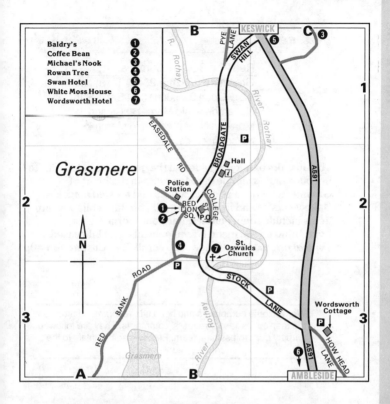

Baldry's ❶
Coffee Bean ❷
Michael's Nook ❸
Rowan Tree ❹
Swan Hotel ❺
White Moss House ❻
Wordsworth Hotel ❼

Grasmere   Baldry's

Red Lion Square, Cumbria.
Grasmere (096 65) 301 ● Town plan
B2 ● Open 10–6 (till 7.30 July–
September) ● Closed Fri (except
July–September) & Mon–Fri early
November-mid March ● No credit
cards.

Paul and Elaine Nelson offer a most appetising selection of daily-changing lunchtime dishes at their counter-service restaurant. Typical dishes include home-baked ham, quiche and ploughman's, and vegetarian dishes range from lasagne to brown lentil cutlets and a deliciously moist, tasty chestnut and mushroom roast. Traditional sweets like bread and butter pudding and seasonal fruit crumble to finish. Throughout the day there are tempting goodies like rich chocolate cake and sticky gingerbread. No smoking. No dogs. *Typical prices* Roast ham salad £3.75 Chestnut & mushroom roast £2.95. WC.

Just a Bite

81

Grasmere *Coffee Bean*

Red Lion Square, Cumbria.
Grasmere (096 65) 234 ● Town plan
B2 ● Open 9–5.30 (10–4 Sat & Sun
November–mid March) ● Closed
Mon–Fri November–mid March ●
No credit cards.

The upstairs bakery provides all the goodies to enjoy with tea
or coffee at this simple little tea room in the heart of
Grasmere. Chocolate cake, scones and toasted teacakes,
Bakewell tarts and flapjacks are all popular, while savoury
items include soup, quiches, flans and Cornish pasties.
Everything on the menu is available all day. Unlicensed.
Typical prices Home-made soup & roll 75p Custard tart 40p.

We welcome complaints and bona fide recommendations on
the tear-out pages for readers' comments. They are followed
up by our professional team. Please also complain to the
management instantly.

Grasmere *Michael's Nook*

79%
£C

Near Ambleside, Cumbria.
Grasmere (096 65) 496 ●
Town plan C1 ● Bedrooms 11;
En suite bath/shower 11;
With phone 11; With TV 11 ●
Confirm by arrangement ●
No credit cards.

Always a pure delight, Reg Gifford's beautifully located
country house hotel is now even more appealing. Major
structural alteration has permitted the creation of two superb
suites and the enlarging of several other bedrooms. Antiques
and stylish individual decor combine with abundant home
comforts. Bathrooms, too, have received attention, some
boasting bidets, twin basins and separate walk-in showers.
Comfortable, elegant public rooms display a superb collection
of hand-chosen antiques, ornaments, pictures and porcelain,
enhanced by lovely fresh flower arrangements. Half-board
only. Guests may use the facilities of the nearby Wordsworth
Hotel. No dogs. *Amenities* garden, croquet, laundry service.

Grasmere   Michael's Nook Restaurant

> Near Ambleside, Cumbria.
> Grasmere (096 65) 496 ● Town plan
> C1 ● Lunch 12.30 for 1. Dinner 7.30
> for 8, Sat 7 for 7.15 (also 9 for 9.15
> Fri & Sat in summer) ● Set L £17.50.
> Set D £24.50. About £59 for two ●
> No credit cards ● Closed Sat L.

This handsome dining room in a country mansion provides a splendid setting for a meal. Daily-changing menus offer imaginative combinations like galantine of quail with haw jelly followed by roast Lakeland lamb with truffles and leek coulis. Sweets are a real strength – try stunning strawberry and plum parfait or chocolate marquise with mocha sauce. Friendly, professional service. ☺

Grasmere   Rowan Tree

> Cumbria. Grasmere (096 65) 528 ●
> Town plan B2 ● Open 10.30–7.30
> ● Closed Mon-Thurs November–
> March ● No credit cards.

Drink in the beauty of the lake before retiring to this chic yet delightfully cottage restaurant for a refreshing brew and some delicious home-baked goodies. Choose from fruity wholemeal scones, crisp almond slice, tea-bread and splendidly moist date slice. Savoury snacks include quiches and jacket potatoes, while at mealtimes there are more substantial offerings. No dogs. *Typical prices:* Lasagne with baked potato & salad £2.95   Cheese & asparagus quiche with baked potato & salad garnish £2.65. ● WC.

Grasmere   Swan Hotel

> Near Ambleside, Cumbria.   64%
> Grasmere (096 65) 551 ● Town plan   £C/D
> C1 ● Bedrooms 36; En Suite bath/
> shower 36; With phone 36; With TV
> 36 ● Confirm by 6 ● Credit Access,
> Amex, Diners, Visa.

A nice old inn with beams, antiques and ornaments bestowing a pleasant, traditional character on the cosy public rooms. Bedroom furnishings and fittings vary, but all rooms offer standard accessories (TV, radio, telephone, tea-making equipment). Some rooms are being upgraded with smart new furniture and flowery fabrics. Decent modern bathrooms. *Amenities* garden, pony trekking, laundry service.

Hotel

Grasmere   White Moss House

Rydal Water, Cumbria. Grasmere	68%
(096 65) 295 ● Town plan C3 ●	£D
Bedrooms 6; En Suite bath/shower 6;	
With phone No; With TV 6 ● Confirm	
by arrangement ● No credit cards ●	
Closed mid November–mid March.	

This delightful old Lakeland house is a charming, friendly
hotel. The comfortably furnished lounge (where drinks are
served) has a restful, elegant air, and attractive bedrooms
feature the odd antique and a full complement of thoughtful
extras, from maps and magazines to hairdryers and hot-water
bottles. Compact bathrooms are well equipped. Perched
some 600 feet above the main house is a two-bedded cottage,
reached by a steep walk or a 1½ mile drive, offering
stupendous views and unparalleled peace. Breakfasts are
excellent. Half-board terms only. No children under ten. No
dogs. *Amenities* garden, coarse & game fishing, laundry
service.

Restaurant

Grasmere
White Moss House Restaurant

★

Rydal Water, Cumbria.
Grasmere (096 65) 295 ● Town
plan C3 ● Dinner only 7.30 for 8 ●
Set D £15.95. About £44 for two ●
Closed Sun (except Easter) & mid
November–mid March.

Superb five-course dinners (no choice except dessert) get
under way at eight o'clock in this charming, antique-
furnished restaurant. Peter Dixon's style is English in the
modern idiom, and our perfectly risen pike and salmon soufflé
and pork medallions with a sour cream, oloroso sherry and
Madeira sauce are fine examples of his skills. The English
cheeseboard is a winner, offering traditional farmhouse
varieties such as Alston, Coleford Blue and Ribblesdale, and
there are some super sweets. Delicious Beaujolais crus and
fine clarets. *Specialities* smoked haddock and hake soufflé,
terrine of sole, salmon and char; mallard with damson, port
and claret sauce; guards pudding with hot strawberry sauce.
℗ ♀ *WELL-CHOSEN* house wine.

Grasmere — Wordsworth Hotel

72%
£C/D

Near Ambleside, Cumbria.
Grasmere (096 65) 592 ●
Town plan B2 ●
Bedrooms 35;
En suite bath/shower 34; With phone 35; With TV 35 ● Confirm by 6 ● Credit Access, Amex, Diners, Visa.

Standing in its own attractive grounds, this 19th-century building provides a warm welcome and relaxed, away-from-it-all comfort. Antiques and fine mouldings lend a Victorian air to the elegant foyer and lounge, while there's a more contemporary feel about the little cane-furnished bar and a conservatory that looks out over the garden. There are also well-planned conference and function facilities. Good-sized bedrooms, individually done out with pretty floral fabrics, have modern bathrooms, apart from one with handsome Victorian fittings. No dogs. *Amenities* garden, sauna, indoor swimming pool, solarium, laundry service.

Grasmere
Wordsworth Hotel, Prelude Restaurant

Near Ambleside, Cumbria.
Grasmere (096 65) 592 ●
Town plan B2 ● Lunch 12.30–2.
Dinner 7–9, Fri & Sat 7–9.30 ●
Set L Sun only £7.95. Set D £15.
About £40 for two ● Credit Access,
Amex, Diners, Visa

Enjoyable nouvelle-inspired cooking in a comfortable restaurant, tastfully decorated in white and gold. Typical dishes range from grilled seafood sausage on a spinach and herb sauce to steamed sweetbreads, crab-filled chicken and stuffed saddle of lamb with rosemary. The sweet selection is tempting, too, with mouthwatering delights like ginger parfait set on glazed oranges or minted white chocolate Bavarian cream with a dark chocolate sauce. Cold buffet at lunchtime, except for Sunday roast. Fine clarets, back to Haut Brion 1961. Service is courteous and professional. ℮

Grizedale   Grizedale Lodge Hotel

Near Hawkshead, Cumbria.	57%
Hawkshead (096 66) 532 ● Map	£E/F
3D3 ● Bedrooms 6; En suite bath/	
shower 6; With phone No; With TV 6	
● Confirm by arrangement ● Credit	
Access, Visa ● Closed early	
January–mid February.	

Peace and tranquillity in a glorious woodland setting. This
white-painted farmhouse was formerly known as the
Ormandy Hotel. Simple comforts are the order of the day – a
rocking chair by the fire in winter; a seat on the terrace when
the sun shines; homely accommodation in fresh, bright
bedrooms with private bath or shower. The nearby theatre
offers varied attractions. No dogs. *Amenities* garden.

Grizedale
Grizedale Lodge, Restaurant in the Forest

Near Hawkshead, Cumbria.
Hawkshead (096 66) 532 ● Map
3D3 ● Dinner only 7–9 ● Set D
£9.50. About £28 for two ● Credit
Access, Visa ● Closed early
January–mid February

Potted trout, watercress soup, succulent roast Derwentwater
duck, old English spiced beef – these are typical delights at
this pleasant restaurant. Margaret Lamb's cooking is careful
and consistent. After dinner coffee or tea is served with home-
made fudge. ☺

Hawkshead
Field Head House Restaurant

Outgate, Cumbria. Hawkshead
(096 66) 240 ● Map 4A3 ● Lunch
12–2.30. Dinner 7.30–9 ● Set L £6.
Set D £12. About £30 for two ●
Credit Visa

The setting is rural and relaxed, the welcome warm, the
cooking English and very enjoyable. Bob van Gulik's menus
(usually no choice) offer six tasty, well-balanced courses, with
typical delights like air-dried Cumbrian ham, broad bean and
lemon soup and chicken breast in a delicate mustard and
cream sauce. Something simple for a sweet – perhaps sorbets
or treacle pudding – then the fine English cheeseboard. ☺
♀ *WELL-CHOSEN* house wine.

Just a Bite

Hawkshead — Minstrel's Gallery

The Square, Cumbria. Hawkshead
(096 66) 423 ● Map 4A3 ● Open
10.30–5.30 ● Closed Fri & mid
December–mid February ● No
credit cards

Teatime is the busiest part of the day at the Russells' charming flagstoned tea room, as William Russell's home-baked goodies come into their own. Sticky gingerbread, scones spread with good jam and cream and delicious meringue glacé with fresh strawberries all go down well with a refreshing brew. At lunchtime, there are a few light savoury dishes such as chicken and mushroom pie. Unlicensed. No smoking. *Typical prices* Chicken & mushroom pie with baked potato £2.75 Mushroom omelette with salad or baked potato £2.70. ●.

Pub

Hawkshead — Queen's Head

Cumbria. Hawkshead (096 66) 271
● Map 4A3 ● Last bar food order
9 pm ● Bedrooms 8; With bath/
shower 4; With TV No ● Check-in:
all day ●Credit Access, Amex,
Diners, Visa ● Closed accommo-
dation only 10 days Christmas ●
Brewery Hartley. Beers Hartley's
Best Bitter, Mild; Guinness; Stella
Artois; Heineken; cider.

(Food, B & B) £F

A popular and traditional pub in a very attractive Lakeland village. The panelled main bar and neighbouring snug provide a fine setting for enjoying some very good bar food, and the promise of the delicious smells wafting from the kitchen are more than fulfilled. Consistency is the keynote throughout the range, from rich creamy mushroom soup and venison pâté to casseroled pheasant, beef curry and some excellent sweets like mocha cheesecake with a super, penetrating coffee taste. Sandwiches are an additional lunchtime offering. *Typical prices* Beef & beer casserole £3.95 Venison pâté £2.55. ☺

Beamed ceilings and simple furnishings bestow an old-world charm on the bedrooms, four of which have neat private bathrooms notable for their generous soft towels. There's a plush, comfortable TV lounge for residents. No under-tens accommodated overnight. No dogs in rooms.

Our inspectors never book in the name of Egon Ronay's Guides; they disclose their identity only after paying their bills.

Heversham   Blue Bell at Heversham

Princes Way, Near Milnthorpe,	*(Inn)*
Cumbria. Milnthorpe (044 82) 3159	£E
● Map 4B5 ● Bedrooms 28; En suite	
bath/shower 19; With phone No; With	
TV 28 ● Confirm by arrangement ●	
Credit Access, Amex, Visa ● Closed	
25 & 26 December.	

Spot the distinctive black and white facade of this former
vicarage, which stands alongside the A6 six miles south of
Kendal. You enter through a small sunny conservatory, and
homely lounges and bars provide ample room for relaxing.
Neat bedrooms are furnished in straightforward style, and all
have TVs, radios and tea-makers. Simple bathrooms or
shower rooms. No dogs. *Amenities* garden.

High Lorton   White Ash Barn

Near Cockermouth, Cumbria.
Lorton (090 085) 236 ● Map 1C4 ●
Open 10.30–5 ● Closed end
October–1 week before Easter ●
No credit cards.

The Georges offer a warm welcome at their Lakeland tea
room and gift shop housed in a converted 18th-century barn.
Throughout the day you can enjoy Mrs George's excellent
home baking – flavoursome wholemeal scones, moist apple
cake, popular lemon fridge cake – with a fragrant cuppa
served in pretty china. Light lunches (available summer only)
feature pâté and quiche, home-baked gammon and colourful
salads. Unlicensed. No smoking. No dogs. *Typical prices*
Chicken liver pâté £1.50   Chocolate gâteau 90p. ● WC.

Kendal
Kendal has always been a busy industrial town; Flemish
weavers settled in the fourteenth century and established
the wool industry and hence the famous 'Kendal Green';
cotton, snuff and brushmaking were later trades that
thrived. Now it is best known for its shoes and for Kendal
Mint Cake. On a hill on the east side of town stand the
remains of Kendal Castle, where Catherine Parr, sixth wife
of Henry VIII, was born and spent part of her childhood.

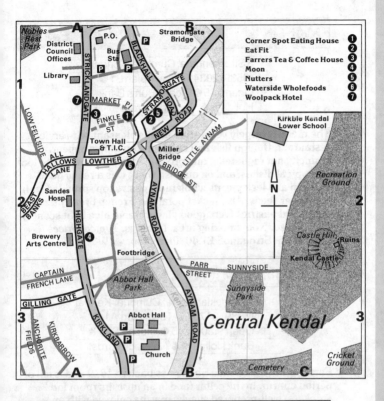

Kendal   Corner Spot Eating House

> Branthwaite Brow, Cumbria. Kendal
> (0539) 20115 ● Town plan A1 ●
> Open 8.30–4.45 ● Closed Sun,
> Thurs & Bank Holidays ● No credit
> cards.

On the lower corner of a little cobbled hill stands this
unpretentious eating house known for its good baking and
friendly, homely atmosphere. Scones, biscuits, apple slices
and lemon meringue pie are just a small selection from the
tempting range, and lunchtime brings a variety of wholesome
quiches. Salads and jacket potatoes are other popular
snacks, along with sandwiches cut freshly to order.
Typical prices Quiche lorraine 85p Haddock & prawn
flan 85p. ● WC.

Changes in data may occur in establishments after the Guide
goes to press. Prices should be taken as indications rather
than firm quotes.

Just a Bite

Kendal — Eat Fit

3 Stramongate, Cumbria. Kendal
(0539) 20341 ● Town plan B1 ●
Open 9–5 ● Closed Sun & Bank
Holidays ● No credit cards.

The menu is largely vegetarian at this pleasant self-service
restaurant, though fish and chicken sometimes appear.
Crunchy nut tagliatelle, mushrooms Stroganoff and lentil loaf
are typical dishes, and on our visit there was a really good
chicken and leek pie, its wholemeal pastry top sprinkled with
sunflower seeds. Also jacket potatoes, French bread pizzas,
cakes and pastries (very good gingerbread, nice light scones).
Unlicensed. Non-smoking area. No dogs. *Typical prices*
Mushroom Stroganoff £1.40 Pizza 55p. ● WC.

Kendal — Farrer's Tea & Coffee House

13 Stricklandgate, Cumbria. Kendal
(0539) 31707 ● Town plan A1 ●
Open 9.30–4.45 ● Closed Sun &
Bank Holidays ● No credit cards.

Farrer's Tea and Coffee Shop goes back to 1819 and is full of
period charm. In the cellar (and in an upstairs room for
smokers) well-prepared snacks may be enjoyed with an
excellent beverage: jacket potatoes are a popular lunchtime
choice, and there's good home-made soup, generously filled
sandwiches, steak and kidney pie and chilli wih salad.
Tempting pastries and desserts, too. Unlicensed. No dogs.
Typical prices: Jacket potatoes with waldorf salad £1.80
Cinnamon & apricot finger 65p. ● WC.

Kendal — Moon

129 Highgate, Cumbria. Kendal
(0539) 29254 ● Town plan A2 ●
Open 6 pm–10 pm (Fri & Sat till 11,
Sun from 7) ● Closed 3 days
Christmas ● Credit Access, Visa.

Warmth and character are all around in this delightful and
popular restaurant. The blackboard dinner menu changes
daily and offers a good choice, for both carnivores and
vegetarians: delicious houmus, asparagus mousse, Italian
lamb casserole, a lovely braised meatloaf served with a super
lettuce and nut salad. Pure, positive flavours abound, and the
high standards are sustained by delicious sweets like Irish
whiskey and orange syllabub. No dogs. *Typical prices*
Broccoli, cheese & mushroom pie £3.05 Meatloaf £3.60.
WC.

Kendal — Nutters

Yard 11, Stramongate, Cumbria.
Kendal (0539) 25135 ● Town plan
B1 ● Open 9.30–7 ● Closed Sun &
Bank Holidays ● No credit cards.

The building dates back to 1670, and there's a wealth of old beams in this friendly, relaxed coffee shop. Savoury snacks on the blackboard menu could include smoked cod quiche, tasty beef and tomato cobbler and baked potatoes with fillings like bolognese or bean goulash. For the sweeter tooth, perhaps lemon meringue pie, coffee cake or sticky toffee pudding. Tea comes in a huge brown pot. Non-smoking area. No dogs. *Typical prices:* Beef and tomato cobbler £2.45 Toffee puddings 85p. ● WC.

Kendal — Waterside Wholefoods

Kent View, Cumbria. Kendal (0539)
29743 ● Town plan A2 ● Open 9–4
● Closed Sun, 1 January & 25 & 26
December ● No credit cards.

Right next to the river Kent, this little vegetarian-cum-wholefood restaurant is a pleasant place to pause for a healthy bite. Our wholemeal pancake filled with tomato and chilli sauce was a very tasty snack, and practically all the salads, soups and quiches use organically grown vegetables. To go with morning coffee there's a good selection of cakes, including carrot, walnut and delicious sticky fig. Unlicensed. No smoking. No dogs. *Typical prices* Vegetable lasagne £1.75 Paradise tart 60p. ● WC.

Kendal — Woolpack Hotel

58%
£D

Stricklandgate, Cumbria. Kendal
(0539) 23852 ● Town plan A1 ●
Bedrooms 57; En suite bath/shower
57; With phone 57; With TV 57
● Confirm by 6 ● Credit Access,
Amex, Diners, Visa.

Pleasant, helpful staff man this old town-centre inn, whose public rooms retain a certain period feel. The best bedrooms are those in the main building that have been given new carpets, brass light fittings and a nice lift to the soft furnishings. Most rooms are in a modern extension, plainish and functional, but certainly adequate. *Amenities* 24-hour lounge service, coffee shop (10 am–9 pm, 10.30 am–4 pm in winter).

91

Farrer's
Kendal
CHEESECAKE

For the base:	50–75g (2–3oz) butter
175g (6oz) digestive biscuits (crushed)	
For the filling:	225g (8oz) full-fat cream
cheese	2 eggs 50–75g (2–3oz)
caster sugar	⅓ pint whipped cream
10ml (2tsp) gelatine dissolved in 20ml	
(4tsp) warm water	
few drops vanilla essence	

Melt the butter and add the crushed digestive biscuits. Press into the base of a well-greased loose bottom 18cm (7in) round cake tin. Separate the eggs and whisk the whites until stiff. Whisk together the egg yolks and castor sugar. Gradually beat or whisk in the full-fat cheese a little at a time. Whisk in the vanilla essence and dissolved gelatine. Carefully fold in the whipped cream, followed by the stiff egg whites. Put in tin and place in the fridge to set, approximately 3–4 hours. When set, carefully remove from the tin. Decorate with fruits and cream. SERVES 8

Village Bakery
Melmerby
PARKIN

225g (8oz) margarine	225g (8oz) Barbados
sugar 225g (8oz) treacle	150ml (¼pt) milk
225g (8oz) wholemeal flour	2.5ml (½tsp)
bicarbonate of soda	10ml (2tsp) mixed spice
5ml (1tsp) ground ginger	450g (1lb)
medium oatmeal	

Melt the margarine, sugar and treacle over low heat and stir until smooth. Take off heat and add milk, then all other ingredients. Mix well and spread into a greased and floured baking tray about one inch deep. Bake in a pre-heated oven 180°C (350°F, Mark 4) until edges are just firm to the touch. Cool, cut and store in an air-tight tin. SERVES 6–8

Kents Bank   Abbott Hall Coffee Shop

Near Grange-over-Sands, Cumbria.
Grange-over-Sands (044 84) 2896
● Map 4A5 ● Open 10–4.30, Sun
2.30–4.30 ● No credit cards.

The warm welcome and commendably high standards of
baking make this attractive little coffee shop within a
Victorian guest house a popular local meeting place. Choose
from a display counter featuring sweet treats like superb
caramel shortcake, chewy florentines and chocolate and mint
squares. Soup, salads and quiches make tasty lunchtime
treats, and freshly cut sandwiches accompany afternoon tea.
Unlicensed. No smoking. No dogs. *Typical prices* Coconut
fudge cake 45p Peanut & raisin shortbread 45p. ● ☙

Keswick

The 'capital' of the northern Lakes, Keswick is a bustling
tourist town. The Moot Hall, on Main Street, was formerly
a prison, town hall and food market progressively, but is
now an excellent tourist information centre. Noteworthy
features are the Cumberland Pencil Museum, which
depicts the history of one of the few traditional industries
to survive in Cumbria, and the Fitz Park Museum, which
contains, among other things, manuscripts of Ruskin,
Wordsworth, Southey and Walpole.

Keswick   Bryson's Tea Rooms

42 Main Street, Cumbria. Keswick
(07687) 72257 ● Town plan B3 ●
Open 9–5.30 ● Closed Sun
& early November–week before
Easter ● No credit cards.

Above a busy baker's shop, this cottage tea room offers an
enjoyable range of cakes and pastries. Strudel, fruit cake and
creamy, featherlight roulade are typical of the choice from
the trolley, and there are set teas – the Cumberland
farmhouse and the lavish Lakeland, a feast of scones, apple
pie, fruit cake and plum bread! Savoury snacks include
omelettes, salads and Cumberland sausage with egg and
pineapple. Unlicensed. No dogs. *Typical prices* Quiche &
salad £2.40 Fresh cream cake 45p. WC.

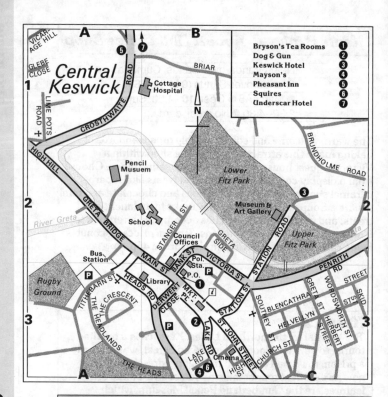

Central Keswick

Key to map:
- Bryson's Tea Rooms ❶
- Dog & Gun ❷
- Keswick Hotel ❸
- Mayson's ❹
- Pheasant Inn ❺
- Squires ❻
- Underscar Hotel ❼

Pub

Keswick   Dog & Gun

	(Food)
Lake Road, Cumbria. Keswick (07687) 73463 ● Town plan B3 ● Last bar food order 9.30 pm ● No credit cards ● Closed 25 December ● Brewery Theakston. Beers Old Peculier, XB, Best Bitter; Guinness; cider.	

Visitors to this characterful town-centre pub will enjoy hearty food in typical old-world surroundings. Cumberland sausage with fried onions in a hot brown loaf is a standing treat, and other favourites include goulash, beef curry and home-roast ham. Lunchtime brings more snack choices – sandwiches, jacket potatoes, ploughman's with excellent Cheddar. *Typical prices* Goulash £3.25 Ploughman's £1.85. ☺

We welcome complaints and bona fide recommendations on the tear-out pages for readers' comments. They are followed up by our professional team. Please also complain to the management instantly.

Keswick   Keswick Hotel

Station Road, Cumbria. Keswick	62%
(076 87) 72020 ● Town plan C2 ●	£D
Bedrooms 64; En Suite bath/shower	
64; With phone 64; With TV 64 ●	
Confirm by 6 ● Credit Access,	
Amex, Diners, Visa.	

A stately Victorian edifice standing in attractive, elevated grounds. The foyer features some grand mahogany antiques, and there's an agreeable bar and leafy conservatory. Willow-pattern china and old prints adorn the corridors, which give access to spacious, well-equipped bedrooms with good bathrooms. Friendly, helpful staff. *Amenities* garden, 24-hour lounge service, putting, croquet, table tennis, laundry service.

Keswick   Mayson's

33 Lake Road, Cumbria. Keswick
(076 87) 74104 ● Town plan B3 ●
Open 9.30–5 & 6.30–10 ● Closed
Mon eve ● Credit Access, Amex,
Visa.

A lofty, modern restaurant with a daytime buffet that offers an appetising choice ranging from Stilton and broccoli quiche to beef or chicken served curried, casseroled or stir fried. Salads are fresh and imaginative, and there are some delicious home-made cakes and sweets. The evening menu is quite cosmopolitan, with a distinctly Eastern slant and some vegan dishes. No dogs. *Typical dishes* Lasagne £1.95 Sweet & sour barbecued fish £4.80. WC.

Keswick   Pheasant Inn

Crosthwaite Road, Cumbria.	*(B & B)*
Keswick (076 87) 72219 ● Town	£D
plan A1 ● Bedrooms 3; With bath/	
shower No; With TV No ● Check-in:	
all day ● No credit cards ● Closed	
25 December ● Brewery Jennings.	
Beers Jennings Traditional Bitter,	
Mild; Ayinger Bräu Lager; cider.	

David and Marion Wright offer a warm North Country welcome at this homely old inn, which stands near the A66 about a mile from the centre of Keswick. Caricatures of local people liven up the bar, where a cheery fire burns. Three modestly appointed bedrooms, all with tea-makers, washbasins and generous soft towels, share a modern bathroom. Patio. Children welcome.

Just a Bite

Keswick   *Squire's*

31 Lake Road, Cumbria. Keswick
(076 87) 73969 ● Town plan B3 ●
Open 10–5 ● Closed Tues, 1st Mon
January–mid February, also
weekdays November–2 weeks
before Easter ● Credit Access,
Amex, Visa.

Call in throughout the day for a snack at this bright, appealing restaurant. Toast specialities are always popular ('For Him' combines sirloin steak with anchovies and olives), and there are lots of sandwiches plus soup and ice cream concoctions. Bigger appetites will go for shish kebabs or perhaps grilled Borrowdale trout. Set teas are served starting at 2.30. More elaborate evening menu. No dogs. *Typical prices* Toast Hawaii £2.30 Shish kebab £4.60. ☺

Hotel

Keswick   *Underscar Hotel*

Applethwaite, Cumbria. Keswick   64%
(076 87) 72469 ● Town plan A1 ●   £D/E
Bedroom 18; En suite bath/shower
18; With phone 18; With TV 18 ●
Confirm by arrangement ● Credit
Access, Amex, Diners ● Closed mid
December–mid February.

Set in extensive grounds, this handsome Italianate mansion enjoys splendid views of Derwentwater and Borrowdale. Public rooms are comfortable, with attractive features including fine mouldings and marble fireplaces. Bedrooms in the main house have smart darkwood units and carpeted bathrooms; annexe rooms are more modest with shower cabinets. All rooms offer many extras. *Amenities* garden, game fishing, croquet, putting, laundry service.

Just a Bite

Keswick   *Underscar Hotel Lounge*

Applethwaite, Cumbria. Keswick
(076 87) 72469 ● Town plan A1 ●
Open 10–6 ● Closed mid
December-mid February ● Credit
Access, Amex, Diners.

An imposing mansion where exquisite light lunches can be enjoyed in the lounge in a setting of great elegance. From delicious soups like brown onion and cider, salads and attractive open sandwiches to game liver pâté with

Cumberland sauce or trout in herb butter, everything is
prepared with skill and attention to detail. Also lovely cakes
and biscuits to have with tea or coffee. More elaborate
evening meals. No smoking. No dogs. *Typical prices*
Elizabethan pork casserole £3.50 Salmon in pastry £3.75.
🍷 ⊛ WC.

Langdale   Pillar Hotel

74%
£C

Near Ambleside, Cumbria.
Langdale (096 67) 302 ● Map
3D3 ● Bedrooms 36; En suite
bath/shower 36; With phone
36; With TV 36 ● Confirm by
arrangement ● Credit Access,
Amex, Diners, Visa.

Local stone and slate went into the building of this modern
hotel and country club enjoying a secluded woodland setting.
The range of leisure activities is impressive, and guests can
relax in style in various lounges and bars (Purdeys, through
which the old millstream murmurs its way, is particularly
attractive). Smartly furnished bedrooms, most with their own
sitting area, have carpeted bathrooms and drying cupboards.
No dogs. *Amenities* garden, sauna, indoor swimming pool,
solarium, whirlpool bath, gymnasium, squash, coarse &
game fishing, discothèque (Wed & Sat), in-house movies,
hotel boat, health & beauty salon, hairdressing, coffee shop
(7.30 am–10 pm), laundry service, children's playground,
snooker, games room.

Langdale   Pillar Hotel, Hobson's Pub

Near Ambleside, Cumbria. Langdale
(096 67) 302 ● Map 3D3 ● Last bar
food order 9.30 pm ● No credit
cards ● Free House. Beers Hartley's
Best Bitter, Mild; Theakston's Old
Peculier; Marston's Merrie Monk;
Guinness; Castlemain 4X; cider.

(Food)

Bar food spans a good choice at this modern pub, part of the
impressive hotel and country club complex. Cumberland
sausage with apple makes a tasty dish, and there's soup, open
sandwiches, seafood platters and lamb goulash. Eat in the
stone-floored bar or out on the terrace overlooking the
waterfall. Live entertainment Saturday night. Children
welcome. *Typical prices* Cumberland sausage with apple
£3.10 Game casserole £3.90. ⊛

Pub

Little Langdale   Three Shires Inn

Near Ambleside, Cumbria. Langdale
(096 67) 215 ● Map 3D3 ● Last bar
food order 8.30 pm ● Bedrooms 10;
With bath/shower 1; With TV No ●
Check-in: all day ● No credit cards
● Closed 25 Dec, also accommo-
dation Mon–Thurs, Nov & Dec &
all January ● Free House. Beers
Webster's Yorkshire Bitter; Wilsons
Original, Special Mild; Guinness
Carlsberg; cider. No real ale.

*(Food,
B & B)*
£E/F

Everything gleams at this immaculately kept Lakeland pub,
whose peaceful beer garden with its own delightful stream is
the perfect place to appreciate the idyllic setting. Eat here or
by the fire in the slate-walled bar, selecting from an
interesting menu (more choice at night) that includes
substantial dishes and Cumberland pie as well as soups,
sandwiches and salads. Tempting sweets, too, and fine
cheeses. Children welcome. *Typical prices* Haddock bonne
femme £3.95 Chocolate roulade £1. ⊝

Pretty fabrics and modern white furniture give bedrooms a
light, airy appeal – enhanced by the bonus of breathtaking
views. One has an excellent en suite shower, the rest share
three spotless bathrooms. There is a chintzy TV lounge for
residents' use. No dogs in rooms.

Pub

Loweswater   Kirkstile Inn

Near Cockermouth, Cumbria.
Lorton (090 085) 219 ● Map 1B5 ●
Last bar food order 9 pm ●
Bedrooms 10; With bath/shower 8;
With TV No ● Check-in: all day ●
Credit Access ● Free House. Beers
Jennings Best Bitter; Younger's
Scotch Bitter, Tartan; Guinness;
Ayinger Bräu Lager; cider.

*(Food,
B & B)*
£F

An agreeable 16th-century inn next to the village church.
Beams, wooden settles and a hearth hewn from local stone
give character to the bars, where tasty snacks like omelettes,
pasties and plaice, chips and peas are served. Home-made
sweets too. Children welcome. *Typical prices* Pasty £1.25
Haddock, chips & peas £3. ⊝

Overnight guests will find adequate if unremarkable comforts
in the functionally appointed bedrooms. Many rooms enjoy
lovely views, and all but two have private bathrooms.

Pub

Lowick Green · Farmer's Arms

Near Ulverston, Cumbria. Greenodd	*(Food,*
(022 986) 376 ● Map 3D4 ● Last bar	*B & B)*
food order 10 pm ● Bedrooms 11;	*£E/F*
With bath/shower 7; With TV 11 ●	
Check-in: all day ● Credit Access,	
Amex, Visa ● Closed 25 December	
exc. accommodation ● Brewery	
Younger Beers Younger's No.3,	
Scotch Bitter; McEwan's 80/-;	
Guinness; Harp, Becks Bier; cider.	

A very pleasant old inn, built about the middle of the 14th century, and originally a farmhouse that brewed its own beer. The bars have a good deal of character, comprising a warren of different rooms, nooks and crannies on several levels. The choice of bar snacks is fairly standard, consisting mainly of things like sandwiches (good ham), smoked mackerel, pâté and steak and kidney pie. Sweets could include lemon torte, fruit pie and sherry trifle. There's an agreeable patio for outdoor eating. Children welcome. *Typical prices* Cheese & onion pie £2 Cold roast Cumberland ham £2.55.

The bedrooms, all clean and well cared for, provide adequate comforts for a short stay. Furnishings are simple and traditional in style, and seven rooms have functional private facilities. There are televisions in all rooms and also a set in the comfortable residents' lounge.

Pub

Melmerby · Shepherds Inn

Near Penrith, Cumbria. Langwathby	*(Food)*
(076 881) 217 ● Map 2C3 ● Last bar	
food order 9.45 pm ● Credit	
Access ● Closed 25 December	
● Brewery Marston. Beers Marston's	
Pedigree; Ind Coope Burton Ale;	
Merrie Monk, Mild; Old Roger	
Draught Barley Wine; Marston's	
Pilsner; cider.	

Very good snacks are served in the cheerful open-plan bar of this well-kept village pub. Daily specials like barbecued spare ribs or delicious ham and mushroom pie are a popular choice, supplementing soups, filled rolls, home-made pastries and good fresh salads. Nice puds and an excellent cheeseboard including Wensleydale, smoked Cumberland and Yorkshire goat's cheese. *Typical prices* Spare ribs £3.60 Cumberland sausage hot pot £3. ☺

Just a Bite

Melmerby — Village Bakery

Near Penrith, Cumbria. Langwathby (076881) 515 ● Map 2C3 ● Open 8.30–5 (Sun & Bank Hols from 9.30) ● Closed Mon (except Bank Hols) & Christmas–Easter) ● No credit cards.

★

A lovingly converted old barn houses this marvellous bakery and tea room, run by the dedicated Whitleys, who provide all the organically grown vegetables, fruit, milk and meat from their own small holding. The imaginative menu extends from super breakfasts to lunchtime offerings of, say, broccoli and lemon quiche, cottage cheese-filled spinach roulade and gooseberry pie to finish. Delicious home-baked cakes and scones, too. No smoking. No dogs. *Typical prices* Creamy vegetable pie £3.50 Trout pâté £1.05. ● WC.

Pub

Metal Bridge — Metal Bridge Inn

(B & B)
£F

Near Gretna, Cumbria. Rockcliffe (022874) 206 ● Map 1D1 ●
Bedrooms 5; With bath/shower 4; With TV 5 ● Check-in: restricted ●
Credit Access, Amex, Visa ●
Brewery Younger. Beers Younger's Export, Tartan, IPA, Scotch Bitter; McEwan's Export; Harp.

This pleasant pub alongside the A74 makes a useful overnight stopping place for motorists travelling between England and Scotland. Four out of the five roomy, attractively furnished bedrooms have private facilities, and colour TVs and tea-makers are common to all. There is one well-kept public bathroom. Visitors can enjoy a drink in the split-level bar whose cane-furnished conservatory overlooks the river Esk. Children welcome.

Hotel

Newby Bridge — Swan Hotel

61%
£D/E

Near Ulverston, Cumbria. Newby Bridge (0448) 31681 ● Map 4A4 ●
Bedrooms 36; En suite bath/shower 36; With phone 36; With TV 36
● Confirm by 6 ● Credit Access, Amex, Diners, Visa ● Closed 10 days January.

Attractive accommodation is offered at this well-run hotel, a

much-modernised coaching inn beside the river Leven.
Prettily decorated bedrooms with simple units have neat
bathrooms. The timbered foyer-lounge and smart bar have a
comfortably traditional appeal, and there's an atmospheric
wine bar and homely TV lounge. No dogs. *Amenities* garden,
coarse fishing, laundry service, mooring, in-house movies.

Penrith

Penrith is a busy, historic market town associated with
Scott, Coleridge and Wordsworth, whose mother's grave
is at the parish church of St Andrew. This church dates
from the twelfth century although it was extensively rebuilt
in the eighteenth. Also to be found in the churchyard is the
Giant's Grave, where stones 15 ft apart are supposed to
mark the head and feet of Owen Caesario, who was King
of Cumbria AD 920–937.

Penrith	Bluebell Tearoom

Three Crowns Yard, Cumbria.
Penrith (0768) 66660 ● Map 2B4 ●
Open 9.30–4.30 ● Closed Sun,
Bank Holidays & 1 week Christmas–
New Year ● No credit cards.

In a tiny bookshop overflowing with volumes, this homely
place is ideal for browsers in search of both a bargain book
and some light refreshment. First-class tea and coffee go
beautifully with goodies like walnut and wheat-germ squares,
cider fruit slice and sticky gingerbread – all baked from
stoneground wholewheat flour and other unprocessed
ingredients. Unlicensed. No smoking. No dogs. *Typical prices*
Cider fruit slice 45p Honey & sesame cake 50p. ● WC.

Penrith	Passepartout

51 Castlegate, Cumbria. Penrith
(0768) 65852 ● Map 2B4 ● Dinner
only 7.30–10 ● About £40 for two ●
Credit Access, Visa ● Closed Sun
Sept–June except Suns preceding
Bank Holiday Mons, 1 Jan, 25 & 26
Dec & late Jan–mid Feb.

The ambience is friendly and relaxed at this agreeable
restaurant, where David Taylor draws culinary inspiration
from all parts of the globe. Typical offerings range from
garlicky snail-stuffed mushrooms and Swedish gravlax to
lamb cutlets with a laver bread and orange sauce. To finish,
perhaps Finnish strawberry soup or chocolate pudding. ℮

Just a Bite

Restaurant

Pub

Pooley Bridge   Crown Hotel

Near Penrith, Cumbria. Pooley
Bridge (085 36) 217 ● Map 2A4 ●
Bedrooms 5; With bath/shower No;
With TV No ● Check-in: all day ●
No credit cards ● Closed 3 weeks in
January ● Brewery Whitbread.
Beers Whitbread Trophy, Mild;
Guinness; Stella Artois; Heineken;
cider.

(B & B)
£F

Spacious bars and a central location with a pleasant garden
running down to the banks of the river Earmont help to make
this village pub a popular meeting place. Bright, good-size
bedrooms have a nice old-fashioned character and share a
single public bathroom; all are equipped with tea-makers.
Residents can enjoy TV in the cosy first-floor lounge. Children
accommodated but not allowed in the bar. No dogs in rooms.

Pub

Rockcliffe   Crown & Thistle

Near Carlisle, Cumbria. Rockcliffe
(022874) 378 ● Map 1D1 ● Last bar
food order 9 pm ● No credit cards ●
Closed eve 25 December ● Brewery
Scottish & Newcastle. Beers
McEwan's 70/-; Younger's
Traditional IPA; Harp; Guinness;
cider.

(Food)

Succulent home-cooked ham heads the list of tasty fare and
the steaks are good, too. If the choice on the bar menu of this
pleasant old pub on the outskirts of the village looks ordinary,
the preparation certainly isn't. Other offerings include soup
and sandwiches (these two are all that's available on
Mondays) and the popular hot pot. The favourite sweet is a
creamy apple gâteau. Children welcome. *Typical prices* Hot
pot £1.75 Ham & chips £2.40 (No bar food Sun eve.) ℮

Hotel

Rosthwaite   Scafell Hotel

Borrowdale, Cumbria. Borrowdale
(059 684) 208 ● Map 1D5 ●
Bedrooms 21; En suite bath/shower
21; With phone No; With TV No ●
Confirm by 6 ● No credit cards ●
Closed early Jan–mid Feb.

60%
£E

High up in Borrowdale, this homely hotel is a good base for

walking holidays. Two pleasant lounges provide plenty of space for relaxation, and there's a cheerful bar featuring photographs of yesteryear's guests. Recent improvements include a neat, new panelled reception. Furniture in the bright, spick-and-span bedrooms ranges from antique to modern, and all have tea-makers and private facilities (one with shower only). *Amenities* garden.

Sandside — Ship Inn

Pub

Near Milnthorpe, Cumbria.	*(B & B)*
Milnthorpe (044 82) 3113 ● Map	£F
4B5 ● Bedrooms 6; With bath/	
shower 1; With TV 6 ● Check-in: all	
day ● Credit Access, Visa ●	
Brewery William Younger's Inns.	
Beers William Younger's No.3	
Scotch Ale; McEwan's 70/-; Lager;	
Beck's Bier; cider.	

Morecambe Bay and the Lakeland hills make a most attractive backdrop for this cheerful inn, which is less than ten minutes' drive from the M6 (junction 36). The bedrooms, all with TVs and tea-makers, have attractive pine wardrobes and chests of drawers; one double has an en suite bathroom, and the rest share a public one. Children are not accommodated overnight, but they are admitted to the pub, and there's a play area. The bar is roomy and comfortable, and when the weather's kind it's nice to sit outside and watch the tide come in. Friendly, obliging staff. No dogs in rooms.

Sparkbridge — Bridgefield House

Hotel

Near Ulverston, Cumbria. Lowick	58%
Bridge (022 985) 239 ● Map 3D4 ●	£E/F
Bedrooms 5; En suite bath/shower 3;	
With phone No; With TV No ●	
Confirm by arrangement ● Credit	
Access, Amex.	

David and Rosemary Glister dispense homely hospitality at this little stone-and-slate hotel, which stands above the river Crake not far from the A5084. A log fire warms the lounge, where there are books for browsing and winged armchairs for dozing; there's also a small, cosy bar. Spacious, traditionally styled bedrooms are provided with radio-alarms and hairdryers; bathrooms are modern. Beds are turned down in the evening, and guests start the day well with a very good breakfast. *Amenities* garden.

Restaurant

Sparkbridge
Bridgefield House Restaurant

Near Ulverston, Cumbria. Lowick
Bridge (022 985) 239 ● Map 3D4 ●
Dinner only at 7.30 for 8 ● Set D £15.
About £40 for two ● Credit Access,
Amex.

A smartly appointed restaurant, where Rosemary Glister's enjoyable dinners are based on select seasonal produce. Hot buttered shrimps or delicious lamb's sweetbreads could precede soup and a main course like poussin or pigeon breast served with super fresh vegetables. Next comes a creamy sweet, then a savoury and good home-made fudge with coffee in the lounge. No smoking in the dining room. ☺

Pub

Talkin Village   Hare & Hounds Inn

Near Brampton, Cumbria. Brampton	*(Food,*
(069 77) 3456. Map 2B1 ● Last bar	*B & B)*
food order 9 pm ● Bedrooms 4; With	£F
bath/shower 2; With TV No ● Check-	
in: all day ● No credit cards ●	
Closed accommodation only 25	
December ● Free House. Beers	
Theakston's Best Bitter, Old	
Peculier, XB; Hartley's Bitter;	
Younger's Tartan; Carlsberg	
Pilsner; cider	

Owners Joan and Les Stewart keep the welcome mat rolled out at this 200-year-old village inn, where decently prepared snacks are served in the simple, traditional bar. Filled jacket potatoes (Talkin tatties) are one of the regular favourites, along with sandwiches, pizzas, rainbow trout and steaks. Daily specials like spaghetti bolognese or chilli con carne broaden the choice and kiddies have their own menu of jokily named dishes. Sweets are mainly of the ice cream variety. The bars are closed lunchtime Mon–Fri except during school holidays. *Typical prices* Barbecued bangers £1.75 Rainbow trout £2.95.

Two of the bedrooms boast fine old wardrobes, splendid beds and good private bathrooms, while the other two are more modern and functional in style. There's a plainly appointed upstairs residents' lounge for those wishing a break from the bonhomie of the bars. Children welcome. No dogs in rooms. Beer garden. ☺

Tebay — Tebay Mountain Lodge Hotel

Tebay (West) Service Area, Cumbria. Orton (058 74) 351 ● Map 4C3 ● Bedrooms 30; En suite bath/ shower 30; With phone 30; With TV 30 ● Confirm by arrangement ● Credit Access, Amex, Diners, Visa.	59% £D/E

A neat modern hotel, part of the Tebay service area just north of junction 38 of the M6. The staff are friendly, the public areas bright and cheerful, and there are views of the stern Cumbrian countryside from the identically decorated bedrooms. Rooms have duvets, lightwood units, radio-alarms and tea-makers, plus compact tiled bathrooms with showers over the tubs. *Amenities* 24-hour lounge service.

Temple Sowerby — Temple Sowerby House Hotel

Near Penrith, Cumbria. ● Kirkby Thore (0930) 61578 ● Map 2C4 ● Bedrooms 12; En suite bath/shower 12; With phone 12; With TV 12 ● Confirm by arrangement ● Credit Access, Amex, Visa ● Closed 10 days Christmas & 1st 2 weeks February.	64% £E

This fine old Cumbrian farmhouse stands in two acres of gardens on the A66, halfway between Appleby and Penrith. Antiques, prints and inviting easy chairs paint a traditional scene in the lounges, and there's a cosy bar and wicker-furnished conservatory. Spotless bedrooms – beams, smart fabrics, more antiques – have central heating, double glazing and neat private bathrooms. Breakfast is particularly good and the Hartley family provide impeccable service. No dogs. *Amenities* garden, laundry service.

We welcome complaints and bona fide recommendations on the tear-out pages for readers' comments. They are followed up by our professional team. Please also complain to the management instantly.

Pub

Troutbeck   Mortal Man

Near Windermere, Cumbria.	*(Food,*
Ambleside (0966) 33193 ● Map 4A3	*B & B)*
● Last bar food order 9 pm ●	£D
Bedrooms 13; With bath/shower 8;	
With TV No ● Check-in: all day ●	
No credit cards ● Closed	
accommodation mid November–mid	
February ● Free House. Beers	
Scottish & Newcastle Chieftain Mild,	
Newcastle Bitter; Guinness; Harp;	
cider. No real ale.	

As far back as the Lakeland poets, locals and tourists have succumbed to the charm of this old inn in a magical position overlooking Lake Windermere. There are two characterful beamed bars – the simpler one echoes with early Westmorland songs of a night. The lunchtime choice of snacks ranges from soup, pâté and sandwiches to salads and a daily special such as mushroom, cheese and leek flan with a jacket potato. Sweets include lemon meringue sponge and a delicious sherry trifle. Restaurant, too. Children welcome. *Typical prices* Chicken breast stuffed with cheese & ham £4 Dish of the day £2.50. (No bar food available Mon eve.) ☺

Traditionally furnished bedrooms – eight with their own bathrooms – offer clean, comfortable accommodation, with plenty of books and a good breakfast. No under-fives accommodated overnight. Garden.

Hotel

Ullswater   Leeming on Ullswater

75%
£B

Watermillock, Cumbria.
Pooley Bridge (085 36) 622 ●
Town plan C2 ● Bedrooms 25;
En suite bath/shower 25; With
phone 25; With TV No ●
Confirm by 6 ● Credit Access,
Amex, Diners, Visa ● Closed
December–mid March.

Built in Georgian style in 1847, this country house hotel stands in beautiful landscaped grounds on the edge of Lake Ullswater (A592). A pillared portico leads into the elegant entrance hall, and two supremely comfortable lounges feature bold colour schemes and fine traditional appointments. There's also an intimate panelled bar. Good taste is equally evident in the bedrooms, which have mainly mahogany

furniture. Magazines, potted plants and pot-pourris are typical
homely touches, and there are good-quality soaps and
shampoos in the bathrooms. Three rooms have balconies,
seven others are in converted farm cottages. No children
under ten. No dogs. *Amenities* garden, coarse fishing.

Ullswater
Leeming on Ullswater Restaurant

Watermillock, Cumbria. Pooley
Bridge (085 36) 622 ● Town plan C2
● Lunch 12.30–1.45. Dinner 7.30–
8.45 ● Set L £5.10, Sun £8. Set D
£22.50. About £56 for two ● Credit
Access, Amex, Diners, Visa ●
Closed December–mid March.

Highly enjoyable eating in a handsome pillared room
overlooking beautifully kept gardens. Simple set lunchtime
meals (more choice on Sunday) give way in the evening to
delicious dishes like venison pâté en croûte or escalope of
salmon with a Noilly Prat, leek and saffron sauce. Fine
flavours and some nice variations on the classical repertoire.
Extensive wine list. ☺
♀ *WELL-CHOSEN* house wine.

Our inspectors never book in the name of Egon Ronay's
Guides; they disclose their identity only after paying their bills.

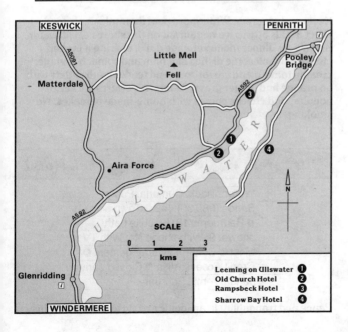

KESWICK PENRITH

Little Mell
▲
Fell

Matterdale

Pooley
Bridge

A5091

A592

Aira Force

U L L S W A T E R

N

SCALE

0 1 2 3
kms

A592

Glenridding

WINDERMERE

Leeming on Ullswater ❶
Old Church Hotel ❷
Rampsbeck Hotel ❸
Sharrow Bay Hotel ❹

Ullswater — Old Church Hotel

Watermillock, Near Penrith, Cumbria. Pooley Bridge (085 36) 204 ● Town plan C2 ● Bedrooms 11; En suite bath/shower 7; With phone No; With TV No ● Confirm by arrangement ● No credit cards ● Closed November–March	63% £D/E

Peace and privacy in a lovely setting on Lake Ullswater. The Whitemores are the most amiable of hosts, and relaxation comes easily in the comfortable lounge and cosy bar. Bedrooms are quite modestly furnished, but stylish fabrics and numerous little extras contribute to a very pleasant overall effect. Half-board terms only at weekends. *Amenities* garden, coarse & game fishing, board sailing, rowing boat, jetty, mooring.

Ullswater — Old Church Hotel Restaurant

Watermillock, Near Penrith, Cumbria. Pooley Bridge (085 36) 204 ● Town plan C2 ● Dinner only 7.30–8.15 ● Set D £14.50. About £36 for two ● Closed November–March.

Kevin and Maureen Whitemore pool their talents to good effect at this attractive restaurant on the shores of Ullswater. Kevin's set dinner menus change daily, offering a limited choice of wholesome dishes like ham and spinach roulade, creamy tomato and carrot soup and tender lamb cutlets with an orange and ginger gravy. Maureen's sweets are very popular, and cheese comes with home-made oatcakes. No smoking. ⊘

Ullswater — Rampsbeck Hotel

Watermillock, Cumbria. Pooley Bridge (085 36) 442 ● Town plan C1 ● Bedrooms 13; En suite bath/shower 9; With phone No; With TV Most ● Confirm by arrangement ● Credit Access, Visa ● Closed early January–mid February.

Peace and tranquillity in an idyllic setting are offered at this friendly, unpretentious hotel on the western shore of Lake Ullswater. Lofty public areas range from the traditionally furnished lounge to the darkwood panelled bar, and there's a smaller function room. Bedrooms have pretty floral prints and soft colour schemes and are nicely kept. Good bathrooms. *Amenities* garden, coarse fishing.

Ullswater   Rampsbeck Hotel Restaurant

Watermillock, Cumbria. Pooley
Bridge (085 36) 442 ● Town plan C1
●Lunch 12–2. Dinner 7–9 ● Set L
Sun only £7.95. Set D from £12.50.
About £40 for two ● Credit Access,
Visa ● Closed early Jan–mid Feb.

Wayne Michael Leadon heads a very capable and enthusiastic kitchen team in this friendly restaurant. The menu (in French with detailed translations) has an imaginative ring, with dishes like prawn and dill soufflé, fillet of lamb with apple and stem ginger, and escalope of salmon with butter sauce and garnish of mussels. Good vegetables and a nice selection of desserts. ☺

Ullswater   Sharrow Bay Hotel

80%
£B

Lake Ullswater, Near Penrith, Cumbria. Pooley Bridge (085 36) 301 ● Town plan C2 ● Bedrooms 30; En suite bath/ shower 26; With phone 30; With TV 30 ● Confirm by arrangement ● No credit cards ● Closed December– early March.

The setting of this marvellous country house hotel is quite stunning, with 12 acres of lovely grounds and glorious views of lake, woods and mountains. Fine antiques, sumptuous furnishings, ornaments and fresh flowers paint a picture of civilised elegance in the lounges, where guests can enjoy afternoon tea or a quiet drink. Bedrooms and bathrooms show the same unique sense of style, combining the finest fabrics and furnishings with countless cosseting extras. Apart from the main hotel, there are rooms in the Edwardian gatehouse and garden cottages, plus others further afield. Half-board only. No children under 13. No dogs. *Amenities* garden, coarse & game fishing, jetty, laundry service.

Ullswater
Sharrow Bay Hotel Restaurant

Lake Ullswater, Near Penrith, Cumbria. Pooley Bridge (085 36) 301 ● Town plan C2 ● Lunch 1–1.30. Dinner 8–8.30. Set L £17.50. Set D £27.50. About £65 for two ● No credit cards ● Closed December–early March.

★

Johnnie Martin heads Francis Coulson's and Brian Sack's supremely talented, long-serving team in the kitchen of this lovely lakeside restaurant where the welcome is as warm and the food as memorable as ever. Their ambitious list of starters embraces cheese beignets and duck foie gras on a bed of spinach while main courses are equally delicious. Faultless vegetables and gorgeous, emphatically British sweets such as butterscotch cream pie and syrup sponge. Lighter lunchtime choice except Sunday. Finely chosen wines. *Specialities* Cassolette of fresh prawns, breast of duck with duck mousseline and a juniper berry, port and redcurrant sauce, best end of lamb in puff pastry with onion marmalade and rosemary-flavoured sauce. ⊝

Ullswater
Sharrow Bay Hotel Lounge

★

Lake Ullswater, Near Penrith, Cumbria. Pooley Bridge (085 36) 301 ● Town plan C2 ● Open 11–11.45 & 4–4.45 ● Closed December–early March ● No credit cards.

To take afternoon tea in this enchanting hotel is undiluted delight: the scenery is unsurpassed, the lounges elegant and civilised, the cakes and pastries impeccably fresh. Scones rise high, sponges are silky-smooth, sandwiches are cut to order, jams are home-made. Morning coffee, which is served with an assortment of biscuits, is an equally winning occasion. No children. No dogs. *Typical prices* Morning coffee with biscuits £2 Set afternoon tea £5. ● WC.

Underbarrow
Greenriggs Country House Hotel

Near Kendal, Cumbria. Crosthwaite	59%
(044 88) 387 ● Map 4B4 ●	£E
Bedrooms 14; En suite bath/shower	
10; With phone No; With TV No ●	
Confirm by arrangement ● No credit	
cards ● Closed January & February.	

New owners have begun improvements at this peaceful 18th-century house overlooking the Lyth Valley. Chintzy armchairs furnish the cosy bar and half-panelled lounge, and an open fire warms another equally comfortable lounge. Bright bedrooms, many with exposed beams, have tea-makers; rooms in the cottage annexe are now linked by covered walkway to the main house. Well-kept bathrooms. *Amenities* garden, croquet.

Warwick-on-Eden
Queen's Arms Inn & Motel

Near Carlisle, Cumbria. Wetheral	*(B & B)*
(0228) 60699 ● Map 2A1 ●	£F
Bedrooms 8; With bath/shower 8;	
With TV 8 ● Check-in: all day ●	
Credit Access, Amex, Diners, Visa ●	
Closed 2 days at Christmas ● Free	
House. Beers Tetley's Bitter, Mild,	
Traditional; Guinness; Skol;	
Oranjeboom; cider.	

A friendly welcome awaits at this popular 18th-century inn off the A69, just a few minutes' drive from junction 43 of the M6. Open fires warm the two convivial beamed bars, and the brightly decorated bedrooms, which are of quite a high standard, are equally inviting. All have TVs, tea-makers and clock radios, as well as up-to-date private facilities. Children welcome. Patio and garden.

Changes in data may occur in establishments after the Guide goes to press. Prices should be taken as indications rather than firm quotes.

Wasdale Head
Greendale Gallery Restaurant

Near Wast Water, Cumbria.
Wasdale (094 06) 243 ● Map 1C6 ●
Open 11.30–8 ● Closed end
September–Easter ● No credit
cards.

A pleasant, picture-filled restaurant offering carefully
prepared, flavoursome fare to suit all appetites. Coffee is
served until lunchtime, when you can have a full meal of, say,
egg mayonnaise or pâté followed by fried plaice, pork chop
with apple sauce or steak Diane, with hot apple pie to finish.
Lighter alternatives include sandwiches, salads and
omelettes, and there's a set tea later. Children's menu.
Typical prices Steak & kidney pie £3.25 Chicken chasseur
£3.60. No dogs. WC.

Wasdale Head   *Wasdale Head Inn*

Near Gosforth, Cumbria. Wasdale	*(Food,*
(094 06) 229 ● Map 1C6 ● Last bar	*B & B)*
food order 10 pm ● Bedrooms 10;	£E
With bath/shower 10; With TV No ●	
Check-in: all day ● Credit Access,	
Visa ● Closed 16 November–28	
December & 19 January–27 March	
●Free House. Beers Jennings	
Traditional Bitter; Theakston's Best	
Bitter, Old Peculier; Guinness;	
Carlsberg; cider.	

Walking and climbing are favourite pastimes around this
splendid inn, which stands in a secluded position at the head
of one of Lakeland's unspoilt valleys. The panelled bars have
a very straightforward choice of appetising fare (there's also a
restaurant). Chicken liver pâté is fresh and well flavoured,
and main courses include cheese and onion flan, chicken
casserole and tasty pies. The platter of local smoked meats is
a popular choice, and a daily-changing selection of sweets
nearly always includes a fruit pie. Children welcome.
Typical prices Smoked meat platter £3.20 Shepherd's pie
£2. ☙

Overnight accommodation (half-board only) comprises ten
comfortable, cosy bedrooms, all with practical tiled bath/
shower rooms and most with lovely views. Day rooms include
a delightful residents' lounge featuring a restored Victorian
fireplace. Good management and staff.

Wetheral   *Crown Hotel*

Near Carlisle, Cumbria. Carlisle	69%
(0228) 61888 ● Map 2A2 ●	£D
Bedrooms 50; En suite bath/shower	
50; With phone 50; With TV 50 ●	
Confirm by arrangement ● Credit	
Access, Amex, Diners, Visa.	

Period character lives on at this updated coaching inn near
the river Eden. Locals gather for a chat in the fishing-themed
public bar, while residents can gaze out over the garden from
the smartly furnished lounge and conservatory bar. Decor is
restful and well coordinated in the bedrooms, which have
hairdryers, trouser presses and radio-alarms. *Amenities*
garden, sauna, in-house movies, games room, snooker,
laundry service.

Windermere

Until the advent of the railway in 1847 Windermere was a
little hamlet known as Birthwaite. From that time on
visitors began to flock to the Lake District and hotels, inns
and shops burgeoned to cater for them. The new name was
taken from the Old Norse name for the lake, Vinand's
Mere.

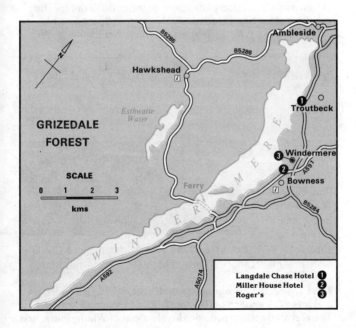

Langdale Chase Hotel ❶
Miller House Hotel ❷
Roger's ❸

Hotel

Windermere   Langdale Chase Hotel

Cumbria. Ambleside (0966) 32201	63%
● Town plan C1 ● Bedrooms 35; En	£D
suite bath/shower 33; With phone	
35; With TV 35 ● Confirm by 6 ●	
Credit Access, Amex, Diners, Visa.	

A fine Victorian mansion in an idyllic setting by Lake
Windermere (A591). The entrance hall, with its oak panelling,
oil paintings and fine old furnishings, has a baronial feel, and
the lounge and little bar are very characterful. Spacious,
individually decorated bedrooms, including six in a nearby
cottage, have tea-makers and remote-control TVs; decent
carpeted bathrooms. *Amenities* garden, tennis, croquet,
mooring, putting, table tennis, rowing boat.

Just a Bite

Windermere
Langdale Chase Hotel Lounge

Cumbria. Ambleside (0966) 32201
● Town plan C1 ● Open 4–5.30 ●
Credit Access, Amex, Diners, Visa.

Splendid teas are served every afternoon of the year. Admire
the lovely lake from the oak-panelled lounge or out on the
terrace as you nibble at dainty finger sandwiches,
flavoursome walnut bread, fat fruit scones with jam and
cream and a selection of delicious pastries (look out for the
excellent strawberry tartlet). *Typical prices* Scones with
cream & jam £1.70 Cumbrian afternoon tea £3.50. ● WC.

Hotel

Windermere   Miller Howe Hotel

63%
73%
£C

Rayrigg Road,
Cumbria.
Windermere
(096 62) 2536 ●
Town plan C2 ●
Bedrooms 13;
En suite bath/

shower 12; With phone No; With TV No ● Confirm by 4 ● Credit
Access, Amex, Diners ● Closed early December–mid March.

John Tovey and his numerous staff provide a warm welcome
and attentive service at this much-loved Lakeland retreat.
The elevated setting provides lovely views of Windermere, and

there's a delightfully civilised atmosphere in the lounges with their antiques and comfortable furnishings. In summer it's nice to join the stone cherubs taking the sun on the terrace. Front bedrooms with balconies provide the pick of the accommodation, but all rooms feature stylish fabrics, good pictures and such thoughtful extras as books, magazines and hi-fis with selected tapes. TVs and telephones are available on request. Private bathrooms (one not en suite) are smart and modern. Excellent breakfasts. Half-board only. No children under 12. *Amenities* garden.

Windermere
Miller Howe Hotel Restaurant

Rayrigg Road, Cumbria.
Windermere (096 62) 2536 ●
Town plan C2 ● Dinner only at 8
for 8.30, Sat 7 & 9.30 ● Set D £20.
About £55 for two ● Credit
Access, Amex, Diners ●
Closed early December–mid
March.

Dinner in this elegant lakeside restaurant is a symphony of tastes and textures artistically orchestrated by John Tovey. The lights dim and the performance begins. Duck pâté or marinated spring fruits could be a prelude to creamy cauliflower soup and an often elaborate roast – our succulent loin of pork featured the flavours of apricot, hazelnut, caraway, Pernod, mint, sage and apple. Add to this the many seasonings and dressings for the six or seven plated vegetables, and the melody is almost lost in the variations. Desserts provide the only choice – we opted for a lovely rhubarb and ginger pie. Smoking not welcome. ⊖ ♀ *WELL-CHOSEN* house wine.

Windermere
Miller Howe Hotel Lounge

Cumbria. Windermere (096 62)
2536● Town plan C2 ● Open 3–5 ●
Closed early December–mid
March ● Credit Access, Amex,
Diners, Visa.

The view from the terrace is one of the finest, adding a magic touch to afternoon tea in this most lovely of settings. The antique-filled lounges are delightful, too, and whether outside or in, you are sure to enjoy the scones and the walnut bread, the lovely chocolate éclairs, the mouthwatering meringues (crisp yet chewy) and all the other delicious cakes and pastries. No children. No dogs. Set afternoon tea £3. ◖. WC.

Restaurant

Just a Bite

Restaurant

Windermere   Roger's

4 High Street, Cumbria. Windermere
(096 62) 4954 ● Town plan C2 ●
Lunch 12.30–1.30. Dinner 7–10 ●
About £34 for two ● Credit Access,
Amex, Diners, Visa ● Closed L Mon
& Sat & all Sun (except Sun before
Bank Holiday Mons).

A pretty high-street restaurant run by a husband and wife
team. Roger Pergl-Wilson's daily-changing menus are full of
good things, from prawn-sauced mousseline of scallops to
saddle of hare, steak béarnaise and breast of chicken with a
full-flavoured mushroom and marsala sauce. Lovely sweets,
fine coffee, delicious petits fours. Bookings only at lunch. ☺

Pub

Winster   Brown Horse Inn

Near Windermere, Cumbria.   *(B & B)*
Windermere (096 62) 3443 ● Map   £F
4A4 ● Bedrooms 4; With bath/
shower No; With TV No ● Check-in:
all day ● No credit cards ● Free
House. Beers Websters; Wilsons,
Mild; Guinness; Hofmeister;
Holsten; Carlsberg; cider.

Set in the pretty Lyth Valley, this unpretentious village
hostelry has been a public house since 1848. There are two
inviting bars, offering a choice of style and mood for the
thirsty. Bedrooms are fairly plain and simple, but well
maintained and comfortable, with full central heating.
Furnishings are modern functional, and the four rooms share
a single bathroom. No children in the bar and no under 14s
accommodated overnight. No dogs in rooms. Patio.

Hotel

Witherslack   Old Vicarage Hotel

Grange-over-Sands, Near Kendal,   61%
Cumbria. Witherslack (044 852) 381   £D/E
● Map 4A4 ● Bedrooms 7; En suite
bath/shower 7; With phone 7; With TV
7 ● Confirm by arrangement ●
Credit Access, Amex, Diners, Visa ●
Closed 5 days Christmas.

Leave the M6 at junction 36 and ask directions to find this
charming Georgian house ably run by the Burrington-Brown

and Reeve families. It's set in quiet gardens and woodland, and the public rooms like the cheerful lounges and intimate bar have a comfortable, homely appeal. Spotless bedrooms mingle antique and modern furnishings, and all provide radio-alarms, tea-makers and neat bath/shower rooms. No children under nine. No dogs. *Amenities* garden.

Witherslack
Old Vicarage Hotel Restaurant

Grange-over-Sands, Near Kendal,
Cumbria. Witherslack (044 852) 381
● Map 4A4 ● Lunch by arrangement
only. Dinner 7.30 for 8 ● Set D
£15.50. About £42 for two ● Credit
Access, Amex, Diners, Visa ●
Closed 5 days Christmas.

The owners share the cooking in this Victorian-style restaurant, where excellent dinners (no choice) are prepared from prime local produce. Mousseline of sole with watercress hollandaise could precede a delicious soup and a roast served with a superb selection of vegetables. Finally come lovely sweets (one hot, one cold), excellent cheeses and coffee or tea. Carefully chosen, good-value wines. Book. No smoking.

Old Vicarage
Witherslack
BLACKCURRANT BROWN BETTY

450g (1lb) fresh or frozen blackcurrants
125g (4oz) mixed fresh brown and white breadcrumbs
125g (4oz) demerara sugar
zest of 1 orange
5ml (1tsp) ground ginger
25g (1oz) melted butter

Place a thin layer of the blackcurrants in the bottom of an oven-proof dish. Then spread a layer of crumbs, sugar, zest of orange and ginger on top. Alternate the layers of fruit and the crumb mixture until the dish is full. Pour the melted butter on top and bake in a pre-heated oven at 180°C (350°F, Mark 4) for about 30 minutes until the top is crisp. SERVES 4

Herbs Wholefood & Vegetarian Restaurant
Skipton
CHEESE SOUP

450g (1lb) potatoes (peeled and sliced)
350g (12oz) onions (peeled and sliced)
125g (4oz) carrots (sliced)
125g (4oz) celery (sliced)
600ml (1pt) vegetable stock
600ml (1pt) milk
275g (10oz) grated Cheddar cheese
salt and pepper
75ml (3fl oz) single cream
chopped parsley

Sauté the vegetables in 25ml (1fl oz) oil to seal in the flavour. Add the stock, bring to the boil, reduce heat and simmer until all the vegetables are tender. Add the milk and cheese. Liquidise until smooth, add the seasoning and cream. Heat but DO NOT BOIL. Sprinkle with parsley to serve. SERVES 8

YORKSHIRE
DALES

Yorkshire Dales

The Yorkshire Dales is an area of considerable natural beauty which has only recently gained well-deserved popularity through the James Herriot television series. The National Park itself covers most of North Yorkshire and a part of Cumbria, and within its boundaries are to be found the typical features of limestone scenery creating some of the most impressive sights in the Dales – the great caves, tunnels and waterfalls caused by the erosion of water on limestone. The most famous is Gaping Gill at Ingleborough, where Fell Beck crashes 361 ft through a narrow gorge into the darkness of a huge underground cave below. At the Ease Gill Cave system in Ingleton there are nearly 31 miles of connecting tunnels and fissures, roaring waterfalls and caverns bedecked with stalactites and stalagmites.

Teesdale, famous for its High Force waterfall, is the most northerly of the Dales. Swaledale and Wensleydale are renowned for their cheese – and linked by Buttertubs Pass! Ribblesdale, along the Pennine way, boasts the splendid 2273 ft Pen-y-Ghent with its huge stone terraces. Wharfedale, the wildest and barest in its upper reaches, becomes exceptionally beautiful further south and Airedale's spectacular scenery includes the 300 ft Malham Cove. Dentdale in the Cumbrian section of the National Park is the quietest and most secluded of the Dales.

The monastic landowners who held sway over the Dales for four centuries laid the foundations of an agricultural landscape that are still to be seen today; the courses of their roads and tracks still survive, and they initiated the building of stone walls to enclose small fields. The monasteries they built in the twelfth century – Fountains Abbey, Jervaulx Abbey and Bolton Priory – are among the most romantic and atmospheric ruins in the British Isles, while at Richmond, Skipton and Middleham remain the great castles of the Norman aristocracy.

Pub

Appletreewick   *Craven Arms*

Atmosphere

Burnsall, Near Skipton, North
Yorkshire. Burnsall (075 672) 270 ●
Map 6A6 ● No credit cards ● Free
House. Beers Tetley's Bitter, Mild;
Theakston's Old Peculier, Best
Bitter; Younger's Scotch Bitter;
Guinness; Carlsberg; cider.

Standing among rolling hills between Burnsall and Bolton Abbey, this slate-roofed pub, some 300 years old, is a splendid spot to pause after a healthy walk. Copper kettles hang from beams in the bar, which is dominated by a huge fireplace. There's also a snug, as well as a garden. Children welcome.

Askrigg — King's Arms Hotel

Wensleydale, North Yorkshire.	*(B & B)*
Wensleydale (0969) 50258 ● Map	£E/F
5D3 ● Bedrooms 10; With bath/	
shower 10; With TV 10 ● Check-in:	
all day ● Credit Access, Diners, Visa	
●Free House. Beers Younger's	
No. 3 Bitter, Scotch Bitter;	
Newcastle Exhibition Bitter;	
McEwan's 80/– Bitter, Lager; cider.	

Askrigg was used as the setting for the television series 'All Creatures Great and Small', and some scenes were filmed in this charming 17th-century coaching inn. The main bar features a huge inglenook and some original saddle hooks, while the panelled lounge bar boasts handsome period furnishings. Bedrooms – with more fine pieces, including several splendid beds – are kept in excellent order, and each has its own en suite bathroom. Children welcome.

Aysgarth Falls — Mill-Race Teashop

Near Leyburn, North Yorkshire.
Aysgarth (096 93) 446 ● Map 6A3 ●
Open 10.30–6.30 ● Closed Mon–
Thurs January & February, also 25
December ● No credit cards

Joyce and Mike Smith run a delightful tea shop at this converted 18th-century mill, where everything on the menu is available all day. Mike does the baking, and his crumbly scones and featherlight sponges, Danish pastries and rich fruit cake are delicious with a strong cuppa. Sandwiches, salads and filled jacket potatoes are also available, plus pies and casseroles in winter. Unlicensed. No dogs. *Typical prices* Toasted waffles 65p Cream tea £2.25. ● ⊖ WC.

We welcome complaints and bona fide recommendations on the tear-out pages for readers' comments. They are followed up by our professional team. Please also complain to the management instantly.

Bainbridge — Rose & Crown Hotel

Near Leyburn, North Yorkshire.
Wensleydale (0969) 50225 ● Map
5D3 ● Bedrooms 13; With bath/
shower 11; With TV 13 ● Check-in:
all day ● Credit Access, Visa ● Free
House. Beers Younger's Scotch
Bitter 80/–; John Smith's Bitter;
Magnet.

(B & B)
£E

The famous Bainbridge horn – traditionally blown to guide
lost travellers – adorns the panelled entrance hall of this fine
old coaching inn that's still welcoming visitors today. The
beamed main bar and cosy snug are full of atmosphere and
there's a larger bar with pub games. Immaculate bedrooms,
comfortably furnished in a variety of styles, offer TVs and tea-
makers; the bathroom facilities are modern and spotlessly
clean. Children welcome. Patio.

Barden — Howgill Lodge

Near Skipton, North Yorkshire.
Burnsall (075672) 655 ● Map 6B3 ●
Open 10–6.30 ● Closed Mon
(except Bank Holidays), also Tues–
Fri in winter & 1 week Christmas ●
No credit cards.

Just off the B6160 between Grassington and Bolton Abbey,
this simple café high up in the Yorkshire Dales National Park
offers a warm welcome and satisfying home-cooked fare.
Lunch and high tea bring hearty platefuls of ham and eggs,
steak or scampi and chips, while for afternoon tea there are
lovely light scones and rich, moist chocolate gâteau.
Sandwiches and fruit pies also available. *Typical prices* Ham,
egg & chips £4.20 Sherry trifle £1. No dogs. ●.

Our inspectors never book in the name of Egon Ronay's
Guides; they disclose their identity only after paying their bills.

Barden — Low House Farm

★

Near Bolton Abbey, North Yorkshire. Burnsall (075 672) 276 ● Map 6B3 ● Open 3.30–6.30

● Closed Tues, Fri, 25 & 26 Dec, weekdays March, Nov & Dec & all Jan & Feb ● No credit cards.

Sensational set teas are served at this delightful working farm, which lies down a steep track leading off the B6160. Super scones, Yorkshire custard pie and a mountain of marvellous cakes and biscuits come with the main course – perhaps boiled eggs, ham and eggs, cold meats or a cheese, walnut and pineapple salad. Minimum charge £2. Unlicensed. No dogs. *Typical prices* Set tea with cheese, walnut & pineapple salad £4 Set tea with ham & eggs £4.90. ● WC.

Changes in data may occur in establishments after the Guide goes to press. Prices should be taken as indications rather than firm quotes.

Bolton Abbey
Bolton Abbey Tea Cottage

★

Near Skipton, North Yorkshire. Bolton Abbey (075 671) 495 ● Map 6A6 ● Open 9.30–6 ● Closed November–March (except weekends in fine weather) ● No credit cards.

Part of the Abbey estate, this cosy, welcoming tea room offers splendid breakfasts worth travelling miles for. Later in the day, equally delicious sandwiches, flans and marvellous salads (with fresh salmon in season) make an appearance, as well as popular steak and kidney pie and big fry-ups. Afternoon teas bring an irresistible array of goodies, from plump scones to moist, featherlight sponges. No dogs. *Typical prices* Steak & kidney pie £2.95 Afternoon tea £2.45. ● WC.

Hotel

Bolton Abbey — Devonshire Arms

77%
£D

Near Skipton, North Yorkshire. Bolton Abbey (075 671) 441 ● Map 6A6 ● Bedrooms 38; En suite bath/

shower 38; With phone 38; With TV 38 ● Confirm by 6 ● Credit Access, Amex, Diners, Visa.

Standing in beautiful Wharfedale, this fine old coaching inn sympathetically blends period and modern elements. The result is a delightfully spacious and attractive hotel: the entrance hall sets a traditional tone with its flagstone floor and open log fire, and the two lounges feature handsome antiques and deep, inviting armchairs. There are two bars, one lively and rustic, the other a cosy residents' retreat. Thoughtfully equipped bedrooms are roomy and comfortable, both in the main bulding, with some splendid hand-crafted pieces, and in the modern wing; all have smart, up-to-date bathrooms. *Amenities* garden, game fishing, 24-hour lounge service, laundry service.

Pub

Carthorpe — Fox & Hounds

(Food)

Near Bedale, North Yorkshire. Thirsk (0845) 576433 ● Map 6D4 ● Last bar food order 10 pm ● No credit cards ● Closed Mon lunch & 25 December ● Free House. Beers Cameron's Lion Bitter, Strong Arm; Younger's Scotch Bitter, Hansa; McEwan's Lager; Guinness; cider.

The village blacksmith's forge survives intact as part of this welcoming pub convenient for the A1. The enthusiastic Fitzgeralds offer some super food, with market-fresh fish a firm favourite, closely followed by such delights as creamy Stilton and onion soup, succulent steaks and chops – and lovely boozy trifle. Service is swift and friendly, and the whole place is kept in excellent repair. Children welcome. *Typical prices* Avocado pear with herb cheese £2.25 Fresh salmon and prawn pancake £3.95. (No bar food Mon.) ☺

Constable Burton   Wyvill Arms

(Food)

Near Leyburn, North Yorkshire.
Bedale (0677) 50581 ● Map 6B3 ●
Last bar food order 9.30 pm ● No
credit cards ● Free House. Beers
Theakston's Best Bitter; John
Smith's Bitter; Guinness; Carlsberg
Hof; Hofmeister; cider.

Once a farmhouse, this friendly North Yorkshire pub enjoys a peaceful country setting. Good eating can be had in the stone-walled bars, with baguette sandwiches a favourite light bite. Other choices include soup, lasagne, deep-fried cod and roast pork with crispy crackling and a decent stuffing. To finish, there are gâteaux, ices, fresh fruit salad and good cheeses. Children welcome. *Typical prices* Grilled gammon with chips £3.60 Lasagne £2.90. ☺

Dent

The historic town of Dent was once more important than its neighbour Sedbergh, but in recent times it has taken a back seat. Situated in the Cumbrian section of the National Park, Dentdale is one of the quietest and most secluded of the Yorkshire dales. Of the town itself, Coleridge once wrote of its exceptionally narrow streets, which at one time were overhung with first-floor galleries.

Dent   Dent Crafts Centre

Helmside, Near Sedbergh, Cumbria.
Dent (058 75) 400 ● Map 5B3 ●
Open 10.30–5.30 ● Closed Mon &
Christmas–Easter ● No credit cards.

An old barn, set in lovely countryside, has been turned into a really delightful crafts centre. In a flagstoned area surrounded by country craft work are a counter and a few tables, where snackers can enjoy an excellent cup of tea and something to eat. Date slice, walnut cake and wholemeal scones are part of a small pastry selection, and for savoury tastes there's a generously topped pizza, with perhaps a soup at weekends. Everything is served on most attractive local Aysgarth pottery tableware. No smoking. *Typical prices* Pizza 89p Wholemeal scone with jam & cream 45p. 🌣 WC.

Just a Bite

Restaurant

Harrogate
Although it is not actually in the Yorkshire Dales National Park, Harrogate offers a host of good places to eat and sleep, and is well worth a detour. Its elegance speaks of its past as a fashionable nineteenth-century spa town; the Royal Baths, which were opened in 1897, were one of the largest hydrotherapy establishments in the world. Now a popular conference centre, Harrogate has every sort of facility on offer.

Harrogate   *Bettys*

1 Parliament Street, North Yorkshire. Harrogate (0423) 64659 ● Town plan C2 ● Open 9–5.30, Sun 10–6 ● Closed 1 January & 25 & 26 December ● No credit cards.

The Harrogate branch was the first Bettys coffee shop (opened in 1919) and, like the Ilkley, Northallerton and York outlets, serves a vast range of really good, wholesome snacks. Rarebits are a speciality, and other savouries include sandwiches, toasties and omelettes, plus grills and fish. Scones, tea breads and a fine range of cakes and pastries accompany excellent tea or coffee. Children's and healthy eating menus. No dogs. *Typical prices* Yorkshire rarebit & ham £3.35 Selection of fruit cakes £1.40. ● ☕ WC.

Harrogate   *Burdekins*

21 Cheltenham Crescent, North Yorkshire. Harrogate (0423) 502610 ● Town plan C2 ● Dinner only 6.30–9.30 ● Set D £7.95. About £35 for two ● Credit Access, Amex, Visa ● Closed Sun (except during trade shows) & 25 & 26 December.

A comfortable town-centre restaurant, where charming hosts the Burdekins offer seasonally changing menus featuring many traditional English dishes. Typical starters might include game pie terrine or lamb's kidneys in mustard sauce, followed perhaps by pepper steak, wood pigeon in a game and redcurrant sauce or salmon hollandaise, and spotted dick and custard to finish.
♀ *WELL-CHOSEN* house wine.

Harrogate — Chimes Tea Room

Unit 9 Westminster Arcade,
Parliament Street, North Yorkshire.
Harrogate (0423) 506663 ●
Town plan B2 ● Open 9.30–5 ●
Closed Sun & Bank Holidays ● No
credit cards.

Fresh, appetising snacks are served in this attractive tea room, which stands on the first floor of an old-fashioned arcade with some fine wrought-iron work. Granary rolls are filled with things like egg mayonnaise, tuna, cottage cheese and peppers or chicken with sweetcorn, and there are double-decker sandwiches combining brown and white bread. Salads, too, plus a good choice of baking that includes coconut tart, date slice and cream cakes. Unlicensed. No dogs. *Typical prices* Double-decker sandwich £1.15 Cream tea £1.40. 🍴.

Harrogate — Crown Hotel

66%
£C/D

Crown Place, North Yorkshire.
Harrogate (0423) 67755 ● Town
plan B2 ● Bedrooms 124; En suite
bath/shower 124; With phone 124;
With TV 124 ● Confirm by 6 ● Credit
Access, Amex, Diners, Visa.

Right in the heart of Harrogate, but quietly placed overlooking handsome Crown Place and the historic Pump Room, this fine old hotel has a lot of character and period appeal. Note the elegant stone facade, the striking, spacious foyer with its intricate ceiling, the leather wing armchairs and chintzy sofas; the pillars are in fact an artful modern addition. There are several bars, the nicest perhaps being the Brontë Bar, an elegant, comfortable and discreetly modern room; on the first floor is a peaceful reading room reserved for residents. The ballroom is particularly splendid, and numerous function rooms amply meet the needs of a conference town. Bedrooms are in the main simpler in style than the day rooms; light and spacious, they have practical contemporary furnishings and very well maintained bathrooms. New since last year are five luxury bedrooms at the top of the hotel with very smart Italian darkwood furnishings and suitably sumptuous bathrooms. Parking is limited. *Amenities* garden, dinner dance (Sat), 24-hour lounge service.

Changes in data may occur in establishments after the Guide goes to press. Prices should be taken as indications rather than firm quotes.

Restaurant

Harrogate   Drum & Monkey

5 Montpellier Gardens, North
Yorkshire. Harrogate (0423)
502650 ● Town plan B2 ● Lunch
12–2.30. Dinner 7–10.15 ● About
£32 for two ● Credit Access, Visa ●
Closed Sun & 24 Dec–2 Jan.

Deliciously fresh seafood is available either in the cheerful
bar or upstairs dining room at this popular restaurant. The
wide range of starters embraces smoked trout and native
oysters as well as more elaborate choices like salmon and
cucumber délice. To follow, try monkfish, hearty seafood pie
or one of several ways with sole and lobster. Less lunchtime
choice. Good Loire and Alsace wines.

Hotel

Harrogate   Granby Hotel

Granby Road, North Yorkshire.
Harrogate (0423) 506151 ● Town
plan F1 ● Bedrooms 93; En suite
bath/shower 93; With phone 93; With
TV 93 ● Confirm by 6 ● Credit
Access, Amex, Diners, Visa.

62%
£D

Although much modernised over the years, this solidly built
former coaching inn on the outskirts of Harrogate retains its
original grand proportions in the shape of an elegantly arched
foyer-lounge and lofty, quietly traditional bar. Warmly
decorated, good-sized bedrooms have contemporary
freestanding furniture, tea-makers and direct-dial telephones;
bathrooms are neatly fitted. *Amenities* games room, snooker,
pool table.

Hotel

Harrogate   Hospitality Inn

West Park, Prospect Place, North
Yorkshire. Harrogate (0423) 64601
● Town plan C3 ● Bedrooms 71; En
suite bath/shower 71; With phone 71;
With TV 71 ● Confirm by 6 ● Credit
Access, Amex, Diners, Visa.

66%
£D

Adjoining houses in a Georgian terrace make up this town-
centre hotel. The Dickensian-theme bar and lounge have a
welcoming air, and there is a pleasant little patio. Neatly
fitted modern bedrooms offer colour TVs, trouser presses, tea/

coffee-makers and good modern bathrooms. The hotel also
has several self-catering apartments. Parking is limited. No
dogs. *Amenities* in-house movies.

Harrogate — *Majestic*

72%
£C/D

Ripon Road,
North
Yorkshire.
Harrogate
(0423) 68972 ●
Town plan B1 ●
Bedrooms 156;
En suite bath/

shower 156; With phone 156; With TV 156 ● Confirm by 6 ●
Credit Access, Amex, Diners, Visa

Extensive, well-kept gardens provide a prime setting for this
impressive turn-of-the-century hotel. The marble-pillared
foyer and airy lounge are on the grand scale, and the Regency
Bar combines period and modern features in attractive
luxury. There are comprehensive conference facilities, and a
new leisure complex is due for completion at the end of 1986.
Overnight accommodation is roomy, traditional and very
comfortable; there are numerous suites, and all rooms have
well-equipped private bathrooms. *Amenities* garden, indoor
swimming pool, tennis, squash, dancing (most Sats Oct–
Easter), 24-hour lounge service, helipad, snooker, table
tennis, laundry service, babysitting.

Harrogate — *Old Swan Hotel*

Swan Road, North Yorkshire.   68%
Harrogate (0423) 500055 ● Town   £C
plan B2 ● Bedrooms 137; En suite
bath/shower 137; With phone 137;
With TV 137 ● Confirm by 6 ● Credit
Access, Amex, Diners, Visa.

An imposing 18th-century building set in extensive grounds
near the International Conference and Exhibition Centre.
White mouldings highlight the gracious light-blue foyer, and
the striking lounge features grey suede walls. Bedrooms –
some with sitting areas – are pleasantly contemporary in
style, and bathrooms are modern. *Amenities* garden, tennis,
dancing (Sat in winter), 24-hour lounge service, in-house
movies, putting, croquet.

NOW ALSO AVAILABLE

IN THE

Egon Ronay's Guide

SERIES

JUST A BITE

PG tips

1987 GUIDE

LIGHT MEALS AND SNACKS TO SUIT ALL POCKETS AND PALATES

Your annual guide to the best snacks and light
meals in some 1000 cafés, tearooms, wine bars,
wholefood and vegetarian restaurants, fish
and chip shops, pizzerias and hamburger places,
coffee shops and many other eating places
serving high-quality food.

**Available from AA Centres
and booksellers everywhere at £4.95
or £5.95 including postage
and packing from:**

**Mail Order Department
PO Box 51
Basingstoke
Hampshire
RG21 2BR**

·S·E·N·D· ·F·O·R· ·Y·O·U·R· ·C·O·P·Y· ·N·O·W·

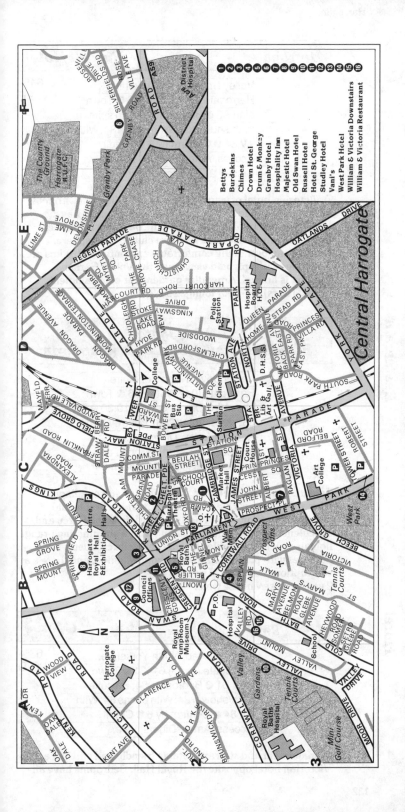

Central Harrogate

1. Bettys
2. Burdekins
3. Chimes
4. Crown Hotel
5. Drum & Monkey
6. Granby Hotel
7. Hospitality Inn
8. Majestic Hotel
9. Old Swan Hotel
10. Russell Hotel
11. Hotel St. George
12. Studley Hotel
13. Vani's
14. West Park Hotel
15. William & Victoria Downstairs
16. William & Victoria Restaurant

Harrogate — Russell Hotel

Valley Drive, North Yorkshire.	64%
Harrogate (0423) 509866 ● Town	£E
plan A3 ● Bedrooms 34; En suite	
bath/shower 34; With phone 34; With	
TV 34 ● Confirm by 6 ● Credit	
Access, Amex, Diners, Visa ●	
Closed 27–30 December.	

A Victorian hotel of warmth and individuality, run with real
friendliness by the Hodgson brothers. The lounge has a
homely, traditional appeal, while the bar, with its leather
sofas and armchairs, offers a more clubby atmosphere.
Biggest and best of the comfortably appointed bedrooms are
front ones with splendid views over the Valley Gardens.
Parking is limited. *Amenities* garden, bar entertainment
(Tues, Thurs), 24-hour lounge service.

Harrogate
Russell Hotel, Hodgson's Restaurant

Valley Drive, North Yorkshire.
Harrogate (0423) 509866 ● Town
plan A3 ● Dinner only 7–10.30 ●Set
D £13.75. About £38 for two ● Credit
Access, Amex, Diners, Visa
● Closed Sat, Sun & Mon to non-
residents; also 24–30 December.

Talented cooking in elegant oak-panelled surroundings.
Richard Hodgson's skills are well illustrated in splendid
dishes like saffron-tinged fish soup, sirloin steak Bercy and
succulent roast Aylesbury duckling with a shimmering orange
liqueur sauce. Vegetables include delicious croquette
potatoes with parsley, ham and chopped onion, and there's a
scrumptious selection of sweets. ☺
♀ *WELL-CHOSEN* house wine.

Harrogate — Hotel St George

1 Ripon Road, North Yorkshire.	63%
Harrogate (0423) 61431 ● Town	£C/D
plan B1 ● Bedrooms 84; En suite	
bath/shower 84; With phone 84; With	
TV 84 ● Confirm by 6 ● Credit	
Access, Amex, Diners, Visa.	

Management and staff are notably friendly and efficient at this
Victorian hotel opposite the Royal Hall. Bedrooms have all

been refurbished, with new carpets and bright modern curtains contributing to the contemporary look. Public areas include a roomy foyer-lounge, two bars and some handsome meeting rooms. Parking is limited. *Amenities* garden, sauna, indoor swimming pool, solarium, whirlpool bath, keep-fit equipment, 24-hour lounge service.

Harrogate	Studley Hotel

Swan Road, North Yorkshire.	66%
Harrogate (0423) 60425 ● Town	£D
plan B2 ● Bedrooms 39; En suite	
bath/shower 39; With phone 39;	
With TV 39 ● Confirm by	
arrangement ● Credit Access,	
Amex, Diners, Visa.	

A pretty patio fronts this friendly hotel converted from a row of 19th-century cottages. The comfortable bar-lounge (which also includes a small reception area) is delightfully homely with its cottage furniture. Compact bedrooms have an attractive coordinating decor and welcome extras like trouser presses and hairdryers in the gleaming modern bathrooms. Parking is limited. No children under eight. Dogs by arrangement. *Amenities* patio, in-house movies.

Harrogate	Vani's Pizzeria

15 Parliament Street, North
Yorkshire. Harrogate (0423)
501313 ● Town plan C3 ● Open
noon–2.30 & 6–11.30 (Sun till 11) ●
Closed 25 & 26 December ● Credit
Access, Amex, Visa.

The pizzas are particularly large and satisfying at this leafy Italian restaurant, a friendly modern place on the main street. Crisp, well-baked bases have generous toppings that include seafood, minced meat and vegetarian with spinach, artichokes, peppers and onion. Besides the pizzas, there's a good list of pasta dishes, plus Italian burgers, shish kebabs, steaks and creamy-sauced savoury pancakes. Starters are straightforward (minestrone, garlic mushrooms, fried calamari), sweets likewise. Service is friendly without being obtrusive. No dogs. *Typical prices* Spaghetti carbonara £2.95 Pizza americana £3. WC.

Our inspectors never book in the name of Egon Ronay's Guides; they disclose their identity only after paying their bills.

Hotel

Just a Bite

Harrogate — West Park Hotel

19 West Park, North Yorkshire. *(B & B)*
Harrogate (0423) 524471 ●Town £E
plan B2 ● Bedrooms 18; With bath/
shower 15; With TV 18 ● Check-in:
all day ● Credit Access, Amex,
Diners, Visa ● Closed 25 December
● Brewery Tetleys. Beers Tetley's
Bitter, Mild; Guinness; Skol;
Castlemaine 4X; cider.

With its pleasant outlook over the green expanses of the Stray
and its proximity to the town's amenities, this up-dated inn is
a good stopover for both business visitors and tourists.
Bedrooms are all of a decent size, with modern furnishings,
light colour schemes and attractive units. Direct-dial
telephones and remote-control TVs are standard, and most
rooms have private facilities. Note the splendid ornate ceiling
in the main bar. Children welcome.

Changes in data may occur in establishments after the Guide
goes to press. Prices should be taken as indications rather
than firm quotes.

Harrogate
William & Victoria Downstairs

6 Cold Bath Road, North Yorkshire.
Harrogate (0423) 506883
● Town plan B2 ● Open noon–3
& 5.30–11 ● Closed Sat lunch, all
Sun & Bank Holidays ● Credit
Access.

A basement wine bar with plenty of character and
atmosphere and a blackboard menu full of interest and
variety. Seafood pâté, moules marinière and garlic
mushrooms make tasty snacks or starters, and our country
terrine was particularly enjoyable – firm and fresh, with
plenty of herbs and a good gamy flavour. Main courses could
include pork spare rib chops, braised beef or poached salmon
with a really good cucumber sauce. Sweets are also very
tempting – try nice gooey banana and caramel pie. Service by
young and attractive waitresses is friendly and unobtrusive.
No children. No dogs. *Typical prices:* Country terrine £1.90
Poached salmon with cucumber sauce £4.95. ⊛ WC.
♀ *WELL-CHOSEN* house wine.

Harrogate
William & Victoria Restaurant

6 Cold Bath Road, North Yorkshire.
Harrogate (0423) 521510 ● Town
plan R2 ● Open 6.30 pm–10 pm ●
Closed Sun & Christmas night ●
Credit Access.

Not to be confused with the William & Victoria Downstairs, this smart, ground-floor restaurant offers a good range of brasserie-style dishes. Eat as much or as little as you fancy – from smoked salmon mousse and a glass of wine to a well-prepared main course such as roast topside of veal, sea trout, beef casserole or roast duckling, followed by a delicious seasonal dessert. Excellent wine list. No children under 14. No dogs. *Typical prices* Roast half duckling with Yorkshire sauce £5.95 Treacle tart £1.35. ⊗ WC.
♀ *WELL-CHOSEN* house wine.

Hawes   Cockett's Hotel

Market Place, North Yorkshire.
Hawes (096 97) 312 ● Map 5C3 ●
Open 10.30–noon & 3–5 ● Closed
end October–beginning April ● No
credit cards.

Morning coffee and afternoon tea can be enjoyed either in the courtyard or in the pleasantly traditional restaurant of this market-place hotel. Sound baking is exemplified by lovely light scones (ours came with delicious home-made gooseberry jam), flapjacks, lemon and chocolate sponges and the always popular date and walnut loaf. The biscuits are delicious, too. Friendly service is another plus. No dogs. *Typical prices* Cream tea £1.60 Plain tea £1.30 Date & walnut cake 50p. WC.

We welcome complaints and bona fide recommendations on the tear-out pages for readers' comments. They are followed up by our professional team. Please also complain to the management instantly.

Pub

Horton in Ribblesdale — Crown Hotel

Near Settle, North Yorkshire.	*(B & B)*
Horton in Ribblesdale (072 96) 209	£E
● Map 5C5 ● Bedrooms 10; With	
bath/shower 7; With TV No ● Check-	
in: all day ● Credit Diners ● Brewery	
Theakston. Beers Matthew Brown's	
John Peel Mild; Theakston's Bitter,	
XB; Guinness; Slalom; cider.	

This whitewashed stone inn of uncertain but considerable age stands right on the Pennine Way. It's a popular place with walkers, who can enjoy a spot of refreshment either in the inviting bars or outside in the garden. For residential guests there are ten simple, but clean and bright bedrooms with a variety of modernish furnishings. Most have shower cabinets. Children welcome.

Pub

Hubberholme — George Inn

Kirk Gill, via Skipton, North	*(B & B)*
Yorkshire. Kettlewell (075 676) 223	£F
● Map 5D4 ● Bedrooms 4; With bath/	
shower No; With TV No ● Check-in:	
all day ● Credit Access, Diners, Visa	
● Closed 25 December ● Free	
House. Beers Younger's IPA, Scotch	
Bitter; Harp; cider.	

Old tree trunks act as beams in the flagstoned bar of this charming village pub by the river Wharfe. In summer, the patio is a particularly popular spot with thirsty hikers and cyclists. Four neat little bedrooms (including one in an attached cottage) share two public bathrooms and provide simple comforts. Children welcome but no under eights accommodated overnight.

Ilkley
Although it is in the River Wharfe valley, Ilkley is surprisingly 700 ft above sea level. A settlement since Roman times, it would seem that people lived here long before; Bronze Age carvings have been found in the area and at Heber's Ghyll there is the Swastika Stone, a carved monument which was probably used in ritual fire worship. Ilkley is probably best known, however, for the immortal song *On Ilkley Moor Baht'at.*

Bettys ➊
Box Tree Restaurant ➋
Craiglands Hotel ➌

Ilkley   Bettys

32 The Grove, West Yorkshire.
Ilkley (0943) 608029 ● Town plan
B2 ● Open 9.30–5.30 (Sat from 9),
Sun 9.30–7 ● Closed 25 December ●
No credit cards.

The menu provides for almost endlessly varied eating at this
attractive, well-run coffee shop, and at all times you can get
anything from a tiny bite to a slap-up meal. Freshly cut
sandwiches, bacon and eggs, rarebits and deep-fried
mushrooms are just a few of the savoury items, and there's a
vast array of fine baking on the trolley. Special healthy eating
and children's menus along with an excellent selection of teas
and coffees. Noteworthy service. No dogs. *Typical prices*
Yorkshire rarebit £3.35 Selection of fruit cakes £1.40.
● ⊜ WC.

Changes in data may occur in establishments after the Guide
goes to press. Prices should be taken as indications rather
than firm quotes.

Restaurant

Ilkley — Box Tree Restaurant

★

Church Street, West Yorkshire. Ilkley (0943) 608484 Town plan B2 ● Dinner only 7.30–10, Sat 7.15 for 7.30 & 9.30 for 9.45 ● Set D £17.50. About £60 for two ● Credit Access, Amex, Diners, Visa ● Closed Sun, Mon & Bank Holidays except Good Friday.

After 25 years of ownership, Malcolm Reid and Colin Long have sold to Eric Kyte. The place is a profusion of paintings, knick-knacks and objets d'art, and there's a talented new chef in Edward Denny. He excels particularly in sauces and seasoning, and his French menus, à la carte or five-course fixed price, are full of interest and imagination. Typical delights could include featherlight sole mousseline, pinkly tender duck with a superb white wine and mustard sauce, and a tarte au citron bursting with natural flavour. Service has a skill and assurance to match the cooking, and dinner is accompanied by live piano music. *Specialities* salade de pigeonneau fumé à la vinaigrette à l'orange, filets d'agneau et sa garniture de légumes, pouding à la saxonne aux fruits rouges.

◁ *OUTSTANDING* ♀ *WELL-CHOSEN* house wine.

Hotel

Ilkley — Craiglands Hotel

62%
£D

Cowpasture Road, West Yorkshire. Ilkley (0943) 607676 ● Town plan C3 ● Bedrooms 73; En suite bath/shower 53; With phone 73; With TV 73 ● Confirm by 6 ● Credit Access, Amex, Diners, Visa.

Fine views of Ilkley Moor are an attraction of this Victorian hotel, which stands in several acres of fine gardens with many mature trees. A modern extension at the front houses a spacious foyer-lounge, and there's also a little bar and extensive conference/function facilities. Smart Italian furniture, quality carpets and pleasant fabrics furnish the lofty bedrooms. *Amenities* garden, tennis, putting, dinner dance (Sat), 24-hour lounge service, croquet, children's play area, pool table, table tennis, indoor curling.

Hotel

Jervaulx — Jervaulx Hall Hotel

71%
£D/E

Near Macham, Ripon, North
Yorkshire. Bedale (0677)
60235 ● Map 6B4 ●
Bedrooms 8; En Suite bath/
shower 8; With phone No;
With TV No ● Confirm by
arrangement ● No credit
cards ● Closed 1 December–
1 March.

Peace, comfort and a warm, friendly welcome are among the assets of this handsome 19th-century house, which stands in eight beautiful acres next to the ruins of Jervaulx Abbey. The entrance hall – period furnishings, paintings, fresh flowers, fine rugs on polished wooden floors – sets a civilised tone that extends into the spacious lounge, where guests can relax with a drink in the most inviting ambience. Bedrooms are individually appointed in attractive style, with pretty pastels and floral fabrics, period or more modern furnishings and lots of thoughtful touches. Inclusive terms only. *Amenities* garden, laundry service, croquet.

Pub

Kettlewell — Racehorses Hotel

Near Skipton, North Yorkshire.
Kettlewell (075 676) 233 ● Map 5D5
● Last bar food order 9pm ●
Bedrooms 15; With bath/shower 7;
with TV No ● Check-in: all day ●
Credit Access ● Free house. Beers
Webster's Yorkshire Bitter; Tetley's
Bitter; Carlsberg Pilsner, Hof; cider.

(Food, B & B) £F

Dating back in part to the 17th century, this hotel stands by the banks of the river Wharfe surrounded by the lovely Yorkshire Dales National Park. Bar snacks, prepared by Angela Rowbottom, are straightforward and satisfying. Local trout is a standing treat, along with lasagne, ravioli and steak pie. Other favourites include robust soups, cold meats, and tasty puds such as rhubarb crumble. Children welcome. *Typical prices* Lasagne £2.50 Steak pie £3.10. ℮

The two bars have a good deal of traditional charm, and there's a cosy double lounge, one room with TV. Bedrooms are nearly all of a good size, smart, with white-painted furniture and nice carpets.

Kildwick   Kildwick Hall

Near Keighley, West Yorkshire.	69%
Cross Hills (0535) 32244 ● Map 6A7	£C/D
● Bedrooms 12; En suite bath/	
shower 9; With phone 12; With TV	
12 ● Confirm by arrangement ●	
Credit Access, Amex, Diners, Visa.	

Standing on a hillside in pleasant grounds overlooking
Airedale, this handsome Jacobean manor house retains
many fine period features. The reception hall with oak
panelling, inglenook and high-backed chairs possesses
abundant character, and there's a comfortable lounge with
plenty of inviting chairs and settees. Attractive bedrooms in
traditional style offer nice touches like fruit and flowers,
scales and shoe polish. Good private bathrooms (not all en
suite). Repair could be improved. *Amenities* garden.

Kildwick
Kildwick Hall, Candle Lite Room

Near Keighley, West Yorkshire.
Cross Hills (0535) 32244 ● Map 6A7
● Lunch Sun only 12–2.30. Dinner
7.30–10 ● Set L £10.50. Set D
£13.95. About £50 for two ● Credit
Access, Amex, Diners, Visa.

Paul Hackett has given a boost to the cooking in this elegant
restaurant with mullioned windows and elaborate
plasterwork. Dishes are classical French or regional English,
with attractive modern presentation. Fish terrine, black
pudding salad, lamb cutlets with mint béarnaise and breast of
Cornvale duck are typical items on the nicely varied menus.
Interesting cellar, including some excellent Alsace wines.

We welcome complaints and bona fide recommendations on
the tear-out pages for readers' comments. They are followed
up by our professional team. Please also complain to the
management instantly.

Kirkby Fleetham   *Kirkby Fleetham Hall*

76%
£D

North
Yorkshire.
Northallerton
(0609) 748226
● Map 6C3 ●
Bedrooms 15;
En suite bath/
shower 15; With

phone 15; With TV 15 ● Confirm by arrangement ● Credit
Amex, Diners, Visa.

Caring and enthusiastic hosts David and Chris Grant make
guests feel most welcome at their sympathetically restored
and historic manor house set in 30 acres of delightful
grounds. Lofty public areas like the striking entrance hall and
numerous lounges (drinks are served in one, as there is no bar
as such) are both comfortable and civilised, with their fine
period furnishings, elegant fabrics and warming log fires.
Good-sized bedrooms – including three with four-posters and
a number with brass beds – are individually decorated in an
attractively light and airy style. Pretty bathrooms with brass
taps are spotlessly kept. Amenities *garden*.

Kirkby Fleetham
Kirkby Fleetham Hall Restaurant

North Yorkshire. Northallerton
(0609) 748226 ● Map 6C3 ● Lunch
Sun only 12.30–1.30. Dinner 7–9.15
● Set L £7.95. Set D £14. About £35
for two ● Credit Amex, Diners, Visa.

The daily-changing set menu features a short but inventive
selection of carefully prepared dishes at this elegant
restaurant. There's always home-made soup to start, then
appetising choices like avocado and tomato tartlets or
brioche with mushrooms. Main courses might include
marinated lamb steak or pork fillet with basil and mustard
sauce. Sunday lunch is sometimes a traditional roast.
Tempting sweets, too such as cinnamon and chocolate
meringue or coffee and almond slice with whipped cream
zipped with plenty of brandy. Everything's home made, from
the good wholemeal rolls to the petits fours that accompany
coffee. Good value is to be found on the wine list, which is
strong in Bordeaux and Mosel.

Kirkby Stephen   King's Arms Hotel

(Food ★
B & B)
£F

Market Street,
Cumbria.
Kirkby Stephen
(0930) 71378
● Map 5B1 ●
Last bar food
order 8.45 pm
● Bedrooms 9;
With bath/
shower 2;

With TV No ● Check-in: all day ● Credit Access, Visa
● Closed 25 December ● Brewery Whitbread. Beers
Whitbread Trophy Cask, Trophy; Heineken; cider.

An attractive and very traditional inn standing in the heart of this unspoilt market town (formerly Westmoreland). Chef-partner Keith Simpson is responsible for the bar snacks that are such an outstanding attraction: subtly flavoured cucumber and cheese mousse; home-baked ham; an exemplary steak, kidney and mushroom pie; lovely pear tart served with whipped cream and tiny ratafias. Other choices include delicious high-quality steaks, or generously filled sandwiches. In the evening the food is served in a simple restaurant; the range is similar but includes one or two specials such as game pie or a fresh fish dish. Children welcome. *Typical prices* Cumberland hot pot £2.15 Game pie £5.75.

Entrance to this fine old hostelry is by a cosy, old-fashioned hall with a fine wooden settle; there are two bars, including an intimate panelled cocktail bar, and a pleasant lounge where residents can watch TV. Bedrooms, approached by a handsome landing with Adam features, are plainish and unpretentious, but with the virtues of sturdy furnishings, soft mattresses and crisply laundered sheets. The two best rooms have simple private bathrooms. Old-fashioned public bathrooms are well-kept. Rise early to enjoy a buffet style breakfast. Friendly staff.

Pub

Langthwaite — C.B. Hotel

Near Reeth, North Yorkshire.	*(B & B)*
Richmond (0748) 84265 ● Map 6A2	£F
● Bedrooms 8; With bath/shower 3;	
With TV No ● Check-in: all day ●	
No credit cards ● Free House. Beers	
Webster's Pennine Bitter, Yorkshire	
Bitter; Guinness; Carlsberg;	
Foster's; cider.	

A friendly welcome greets all who make it to this simple little 17th-century inn high up in picturesque Arkengarthdale, an exceptionally pretty little dale, a mile from Langthwaite. The cheerful beamed bar with its barrel tables has a separate section with a pool table, and the homely residents' lounge offers plenty of space for relaxation. Modest bedrooms – all equipped with tea-makers – are bright and clean. The simple bathrooms are clean and adequate with white suites. One room has a bathroom en suite, two others have shower cubicles. No dogs in rooms. Patio.

Our inspectors never book in the name of Egon Ronay's Guides; they disclose their identity only after paying their bills.

Pub

Malham — Buck Inn

Near Skipton, North Yorkshire.	*(B & B)*
Airton (072 93) 317 ● Map 5D6 ●	£F
Bedrooms 10; With bath/shower 4;	
With TV 1 ● Check-in: all day ●	
No credit cards ● Free House.	
Beers Theakston's Bitter, XB, Old	
Peculier; Younger's Scotch Bitter;	
Guinness; Kestrel; cider.	

Walkers and tourists in the lovely Yorkshire Dales find this sturdy stone inn a good place to pause, whether for a refreshing drink or an overnight stay. Day rooms include a delightful main bar with a real feel of the area, a busy walkers' bar and a residents' lounge with TV. Some handsome pieces of period furniture may be found in the good-sized bedrooms, all of which have duvets and the facility for making your own tea or coffee. Four of the rooms have modern and functional private bath or shower. Remaining rooms share two well-kept bathrooms. The landlady, Mrs Robinson, is particularly friendly and helpful. Children welcome.

143

Hotel

Markington *Hob Green Hotel*

71%
£D

Near Harrogate, North
Yorkshire. Harrogate (0423)
770031 ● Map 6C6 ●
Bedrooms 12; En suite bath/
shower 12; With phone 12;
With TV 12 ● Confirm by
arrangement ● Credit Access,
Amex, Diners, Visa.

Surrounded by beautifully kept grounds, with magnificent
views of the rolling Yorkshire countryside, this stylishly
converted country mansion offers peace and tranquillity
combined with friendly, courteous service. Fresh flowers
grace spacious public areas like the comfortable foyer and
drawing room, both of which boast elegant floral wallpaper,
fine period furnishings and log fires in winter. On fine days,
the airy sun lounge is a favourite retreat. Individually
decorated bedrooms (many with lovely outlooks) all have
mini-bars, hairdryers, tissues and tea-makers. Tiled
bathrooms are equally thoughtfully equipped. Helpful staff.
Amenities garden, croquet, laundry service.

Pub

Middleham *Black Swan*

Market Place, North Yorkshire.
Wensleydale (0969) 22221 ● Map
6B3 ● Bedrooms 7; With bath/
shower 7; With TV 7 ● Check-in: all
day ● No credit cards ● Closed 24,
25 & 26 December ● Free House.
Beers Theakson's Best Bitter, Old
Peculier; John Smith's Bitter, Lager;
Guinness; Carlsberg; cider.

(B & B)
£F

Middleham is a long-established centre of racehorse training,
so the pictures and paraphernalia in the bar of this 17th-
century inn are appropriately horsey. The bar itself is full of
country charm, and summer sipping can be enjoyed in a
pleasant garden. Bedrooms are very neat and tidy; four have
original beams, and furnishings vary from traditional (two
have four-posters) to modern in three more compact rooms.
Children welcome but no under-fives accommodated
overnight.

Moulton
Black Bull Inn

Near Richmond, North Yorkshire.
(Food)
★

Barton (032 577) 289 ● Map 6C2 ●

Last bar food order ? pm ● Credit

Access, Amex, Visa ● Closed 1

week Christmas ● Free house.

Beers Theakston's Best Bitter;

Carlsberg Hof.

People come from miles around to enjoy the excellent lunchtime snacks at this modest but welcoming pub with its pew-seated beamed bar. Tuck into home-made soups (our asparagus was excellent), jumbo sausages, Welsh rarebit, spare ribs, or a dish of super gnocchi provençale. There are salads and sandwiches (prawns and smoked salmon are popular ingredients), pâté, and for afters, excellent cheeses and the famous cream-filled brandy snaps. The full restaurant menu is also available, except for Saturday lunchtime and all day Sunday (see next entry). Children welcome. *Typical bar prices* Prawn salad £2.75 Spare ribs £3 (No bar food eves or Sun). ❸

Moulton
Black Bull Inn Restaurant

Near Richmond, North Yorkshire.

Barton (032 577) 289 ● Map 6C2 ●

Lunch 12–2, Dinner 7–10.15, Sat 7–

10.30 ● Set L £7. About £38 for

two ● Credit Access, Amex, Visa ●

Closed L Sat, all Sun & one week

Christmas.

From the outside, a low white-painted village pub, but once inside you'll find quite a large-scale catering operation. Much of the trade comes from loyal and enthusiastic regulars, and there's also a good deal of business entertaining. There's a series of dining areas, including a converted Pullman car from the *Brighton Belle*. The main menu strongly features fish; tasty ways with sole, scallops and trout are popular choices, as well as oysters, lobster, Dublin Bay prawns and paella. Also plenty of choice for carnivores, plus abundant tempting starters. Delicious cream-filled brandy snaps or pancakes for afters. Simpler and shorter lunchtime menu. ❸
♀ *WELL-CHOSEN* house wine.

Just a Bite

Otley — Chatters Tea Shoppe

3 Bayhorse Court, Otley, West
Yorkshire. Otley (0294) 466691 ●
Map 6C7 ● Open 10–4.30
(till 5 Sat & daily in summer) Sun 2–
5.30 ● Closed Sun October–
April, August Bank Holiday & 24
December–2 January ● No credit
cards.

Set in an attractive courtyard just off the main road through town, this welcoming tea shop done up in Victorian style offers a simple but appealing bill of fare. The local cured ham is a great favourite, as the basis of a salad or in a sandwich, omelette or jacket potato. There's also soup, pâté and a selection of baking and gâteaux. Teas are available in many varieties, including lemon and orange, passion fruit and jasmin blossom. Cream teas. Unlicensed. No dogs *Typical prices* Gammon & eggs £2.20 Quiche lorraine £1.75. ● WC.

Hotel

Otley — Chevin Lodge

York Gate, West Yorkshire. Otley   67%
(0943) 467818 ● Map 6C7 ●   £D
Bedrooms 37; En suite bath/shower
37; With phone 37; With TV 28
● Confirm by 6 ● Credit
Access, Amex, Visa.

This hospitable complex of Scandinavian pine on the edge of the Yorkshire Dales makes a delightfully different place to stay. The main building houses comfortable lounge and bar areas, plus 18 bedrooms (some with balconies or patios). Duvets and pine walls establish the decorative theme, and carpeted bathrooms are modern. Other rooms are in lodges scattered about the extensive estate, which comprises 50 wooded acres with three man-made lakes. *Amenities* garden, coarse & game fishing.

Changes in data may occur in establishments after the Guide goes to press. Prices should be taken as indications rather than firm quotes.

Pateley Bridge — Willow

Park Road, North Yorkshire.
Pateley Bridge (0423) 711689 ●
Map 6B5 ● Open noon–2 & 6.30–
9.30 ● Closed Sun eve, all Mon,
Tues, Bank Holidays (except Good
Fri & 25 December) & 2 weeks
February ● Credit Access, Amex,
Visa.

New owners Mervyn and Kate Naylor are retaining many tried
and tested favourites from the previous owners' menu at this
neat, beamed restaurant. Dishes like choux pastry filled with
prawns in garlic mayonnaise or smoked oyster and bacon
kebabs make deliciously different snacks or starters, while
main courses such as chicken in a creamy lemon sauce or
pork fillet with apple stuffing in puff pastry provide plenty of
interest. Tempting sweets include chocolate and brandy fudge
cake and well-made Danish apple pie. No dogs. *Typical
prices* Grouse in red wine & herb sauce £7.25 Smoked oyster
& bacon kebabs £2.25. ● WC.

We welcome complaints and bona fide recommendations on
the tear-out pages for readers' comments. They are followed
up by our professional team. Please also complain to the
management instantly.

Pickhill — Nag's Head

(B & B)
£F

Near Thirsk, North Yorkshire.
Thirsk (0845) 567391 ● Map 6D4 ●
Bedrooms 10; With bath/shower 10;
With TV 10 ● Check-in: all day ●
Credit Access, Visa ● Free House.
Beers Theakston's Best Bitter, Old
Peculier, XB; Tetley's Bitter;
Carlsberg Hof; Slalom Pilsner; cider.

A popular inn situated in an unspoilt North Yorkshire village
about 1½ miles from the A1. Behind a fairly stark and
angular exterior are two pleasant bars (one featuring an
impressive collection of neckties) and a recently constructed
extension with a flagstoned hallway and a proper reception
area. Eight of the bedrooms are in the main building, the
other two in a separate cottage. All have duvets, decent pine
furniture, colour TVs, digital radio-alarms, tea-making
facilities and good modern showers or bathrooms. Central
heating keeps things cosy. Children welcome.

Pub

Restaurant

Pool-in-Wharfedale
Pool Court

★

Near Otley, West Yorkshire. Arthington (0532) 842288 ● Map 6C7 ● Lunch by arrangement only. Dinner 7–10 ● Set D from £10. About £52 for two ● Credit Access, Amex, Diners, Visa ● Closed Sun, Mon, 2 weeks July/August & 25 December–7 January

A splendidly elegant dining room where superb cooking is matched by service that combines high professionalism with genuine friendliness. Chef Melvin Jordan uses impeccable ingredients in dishes of consistent excellence, from mushroom consommé and Jerusalem artichoke mousse to memorable chicken and scampi served on vermicelli, the sauce glazed with a perfect hollandaise. *Specialities* Dover sole with a mousse of sea trout, roast saddle of hare, calf's liver with sweetbreads and kidneys.

⌑ *OUTSTANDING* ♀ *WELL-CHOSEN* house wine

Bedrooms 4; With bath/ shower 4.	£ B/C

Beautifully decorated bedrooms are luxuriously equipped, with TVs, bar fridges, wall safes and direct-dial phones. Each room is decorated in its own distinctive style. Long-standing, friendly and enthusiastic staff help to provide a relaxed atmosphere, combined with very personal service. Diners only. No dogs.

We welcome complaints and bona fide recommendations on the tear-out pages for readers' comments. They are followed up by our professional team. Please also complain to the management instantly.

Ripon

A small market town on the River Ure, Ripon believes in maintaining its traditions: every night at 9 pm, the Wakeman blows a horn, a custom that goes back 1000 years when this signalled the beginning of the Wakeman's nightly vigil. Its twelfth-century cathedral is on the site of an Anglo-Saxon church, of which only the crypt remains. Three miles to the south-west of the town are the beautiful ruins of Fountains Abbey.

Ripon	Ripon Spa Hotel	
Park Street, North Yorkshire. Ripon	63%	
(0765) 2172 ● Map 6D5 ●	£E	
Bedrooms 41; En suite bath/shower		
41; With phone 41; With TV 41 ●		
Confirm by 6 ● Credit Access,		
Amex, Diners, Visa.		

Old-fashioned standards of service distinguish this turn-of-the-century hotel in a quiet setting yet not far from the city centre. Lofty public areas include a smart cocktail bar and airy garden lounge. Prettily decorated bedrooms of varying size have direct-dial telephones, tea-makers and neat bathrooms offering lovely big towels. *Amenities* garden, dancing (Sat monthly Sept–May), pool table, laundry service, giant chess.

Ripon	Unicorn Hotel	
Market Place, North Yorkshire.	(B & B)	
Ripon (0765) 2202 ● Map 6D5 ●	£E/F	
Bedrooms 27; With bath/shower 27;		
With TV 27 ● Check-in: all day ●		
Credit access, Amex, Diners, Visa ●		
Closed 24 & 25 December ● Free		
House. Beers Theakston's Best		
Bitter, XB; John Smith's Bitter;		
Youngers Scotch Bitter; Guinness;		
Carlsberg Export; cider.		

An old posting house standing in the market place of a historic city that was granted its first charter 1100 years ago. The public bar is a favourite meeting place for the locals, and there's a comfortable lounge bar along with a residents' lounge. Bedrooms are light, spacious and quite well equipped (TVs, tea-makers, direct-dial telephones). Adequate private bath or shower in every room. Children welcome.

Hotel

Pub

149

Ripon · Warehouse

Court Terrace, Kirkgate, North
Yorkshire. Ripon (0765) 4665 ●
Map 6D5 ● Open 9.30–5.15
● Closed Sun, 1 January, 1 May &
25 & 26 December ● No credit
cards.

A bewildering selection of enticing dishes is laid out at this friendly, stylish restaurant above a craft shop. Help yourself to tasty wholemeal flans, crisp salads and gorgeous cakes – from caramel shortbread to walnut and chocolate sponges. Lunchtime brings home-made soups and delicious hot dishes like minted cucumber lamb, cottage pie and chicken with peaches. Non-smoking areas. No dogs. *Typical prices* Minted lamb with potatoes & vegetables £2.95 Strawberry meringue gâteau 95p. ● ⊝

Risplith · Black-a-Moor Inn

(B & B)
£F

Near Ripon, North Yorkshire.
Sawley (075 586) 214 ● Map 6C5
● Bedrooms 3; With bath/shower No;
With TV No ● Check-in: all day
● Credit Access, Amex, Diners, Visa
● Free House. Beers John Smith's
Bitter, Bright Bitter; Younger's
Scotch Bitter; Hofmeister; cider.

A pretty stone-built pub located on the B6265 about five miles west of Ripon. It's a good spot for an overnight stop and the three bedrooms are all of quite a decent size; they share a neat, functional bathroom. The single spacious bar is divided into public (games and jukebox) and plusher lounge areas. Pub closed Monday lunchtime except for Bank Holidays. No children in the bar and no under 15s accommodated overnight. No dogs in rooms. Garden.

Settle · Car & Kitchen

Market Place, North Yorkshire.
Settle (072 92) 3638 ● Map 5C6 ●
Open 9.30–5 (Sun from 11) ●
Closed 1 January & 25 & 26
December ● No credit cards.

This pleasant little upstairs coffee shop is a convivial spot for enjoying a snack. Morning coffee and afternoon tea come with some fine baking, from scones and flapjacks to lemon bread or date and walnut loaf. Lunchtime (no smoking) heralds an interesting savoury choice that could include quiche, meatloaf and aubergine parmesan. Filled jacket potatoes are popular, and you might finish with a nice fruit crumble. Unlicensed. No dogs. *Typical prices* Aubergine Parmesan £2.25 Curried chicken mayonnaise £2.20. WC.

Skipton

Skipton stands at the most northerly point of the 130-mile Leeds and Liverpool canal, which was opened in 1816. Although it has been extensively concerned with the textile industry, Skipton is nevertheless green and rural and is an excellent base for exploring the dales. The castle, former home of the Clifford family, dates from the fourteenth century, although it was partially destroyed in 1649 and subsequently rebuilt by Lady Anne Clifford.

Skipton
Herbs Wholefood & Vegetarian Restaurant

★

10 High Street, North Yorkshire. Skipton (0756) 60619 ● Map 5D7 ● Open 9.30–5 ● Closed Sun, Tues & 25 & 26 December ● No credit cards.

Superb ingredients, careful preparation, keen service and spotless surroundings make this restaurant above a wholefood shop a delightful must to visit. The eating area is simply furnished with pine tables and benches, and a display cabinet separates the restaurant from the little kitchen. Lunchtimes are especially rewarding, with appetising choices ranging from egg and sage pâté, marvellous wine-cooked ratatouille and spinach, mushrooms and rice in cheese sauce to a popular fruit and nut platter and lovely salads. Super sweets throughout the day include Swedish applecake, chocolate gâteau and treacle tart. Unlicensed. No dogs. *Typical prices* Cheese & onion pie with salad £2.25 Vegetable pancakes with hazelnut sauce £2.45. WC.

Starbotton   Fox & Hounds

Atmosphere

Near Kettlewell, Upper Wharfdale,
North Yorkshire. Kettlewell (075
676) 269 ● Map 5D5 ● Credit
Access, Visa ● Free House. Beers
Theakston's Best Bitter, Old
Peculier, XB; Younger's Scotch
Bitter; Carlsberg, Taylor's Best
Bitter, Landlord; cider.

A typical little Yorkshire Dales pub, where you can expect a friendly welcome from the owners, the Wilkinsons. The exterior is smartly painted white, and inside there's a tiny bar with a splendid open fireplace, flagstone floor, rough stone walls and a motley collection of rustic furniture. Children welcome. Garden.

Sutton Howgrave   White Dog Inn

Near Ripon, North Yorkshire.	(Food)
Melmerby (076 584) 404 ● Map 6D4	
● Last bar food order 2 pm ● No	
credit cards ● Closed Mon & eve 25	
December ● Free House. Beers	
Webster's Pennine Bitter; Carlsberg	
Hof. No real ale.	

Lunchtime snacks are full of variety at this pleasant village pub named in memory of a beloved bull terrier. Cooking is robust and dependable, with things like venison pie, mariner's hot pot and chicken casserole among the stalwarts. Also sandwiches and salads, omelettes, steaks and sweets. Restaurant meals in the evening. Children welcome. *Typical prices* Mariner's hot pot £2.50 Iced rum truffle £1.25. (No bar food eves). Garden. ⊖

Threshfield   Wilson Arms Hotel

Near Skipton, North Yorkshire.	62%
Grassington (0756) 752666 ● Map	£D/E
5D6 ● Bedrooms 28; En suite bath/	
shower 28; With phone 28 ● With	
TV 28 ● Confirm by arrangement ●	
Credit Access, Amex, Diners, Visa.	

Excellent standards of housekeeping and an ideal position for exploring the Yorkshire Dales are double attractions of this much-extended Edwardian hotel. An open fire warms the

little foyer-lounge, which, like the cosy bars, has quaint
stained-glass windows, and a comfortable lounge overlooks
the wooded garden. Bright, spacious bedrooms have fitted
units, tea-makers and spotless bathrooms. *Amenities* garden,
game fishing, croquet.

Wath-in-Nidderdale   Sportsman's Arms

Pub

	(Food, B & B) £E/F
Pateley Bridge, Near Harrogate, North Yorkshire. Harrogate (0423) 711306 ● Map 6B5 ● Last bar food order 2 pm ● Bedrooms 6; With bath/ shower 2; With TV No ● Check-in: all day ● Credit Access, Amex, Diners, Visa ● Closed accommodation 24, 25 & 26 December ● Free House. Beers Theakston's Bitter; Younger's Scotch Bitter; McEwan's Export; Guinness; Carlsberg Hof; Harp; cider. No real ale.	

The river Nidd runs not a hundred yards from this handsome
sandstone hotel, which stands in an area of great natural
beauty just a quarter of a mile from Gouthwaite Reservoir,
famous for its birdlife. Enjoyable snacks may be ordered in
the bar between noon and 2; there's also a restaurant with à
la carte and prix fixe menus. Soup, pâté and ploughman's,
garlic prawns, rarebit and pasta are typical snacks, or you can
push the boat out with the day's fish special, perhaps
monkfish with Chablis sauce, or a sirloin steak. Sweets
provide less interest. Children welcome. *Typical prices*
Nidderdale trout meunière £3.25 Creamed garlic
mushrooms with bacon & crusty bread £2.50 (No bar food
eves). ☺

Bedrooms, all of a decent size, are kept very neat and tidy.
Attractive pine furnishings and pretty floral fabrics take the
eye, and two rooms have their own attractive and functional
bathrooms. Besides the simply appointed bar there's a
comfortable lounge and a homely TV room, and the garden is
set for summer sipping.

Changes in data may occur in establishments after the Guide
goes to press. Prices should be taken as indications rather
than firm quotes.

Pub

West Witton   *Wensleydale Heifer*

Near Leyburn, North Yorkshire.   *(B & B)*
Wensleydale (0969) 22322 ● Map   £E
6A3 ● Bedrooms 20; With bath/
shower 20; With TV 20 ● Check-in:
all day ● Credit Access, Amex, Visa
● Free House. Beers Younger's IPA;
McEwan's Export, Lager; Stella
Artois; cider.

Set among splendid Wensleydale scenery on the A684
Leyburn–Hawes Road, this 17th-century inn is a comfortable
base for tourists and walkers. Half the bedrooms are in the
main building, the rest in adjacent premises; decor is quietly
appealing, and furnishings range from modern fitted to
attractive period. TVs and tea-makers are standard, and all
rooms have en suite shower or bathroom. Charming bar,
inviting lounge. Children welcome.

INDEX

NOW ALSO AVAILABLE

—— IN THE ——
Egon Ronay's Guide
—— SERIES ——

MINUTES
FROM THE MOTORWAY

M25

AROUND LONDON GUIDE TO
FOOD AND ACCOMMODATION

☐

Newly compiled for 1987,
this colourful guide spotlights over 200
carefully selected eating places within easy
reach of London's orbital motorway.

☐

Everything from starred restaurants and country
pubs to the best tearooms and wine bars.

☐

Special features include detailed area maps

**Available from AA Centres
and booksellers everywhere at £5.95
or £6.95 including postage
and packing from:**

**Mail Order Department
PO Box 51
Basingstoke
Hampshire
RG21 2BR**

·S·E·N·D·F·O·R·Y·O·U·R·C·O·P·Y·N·O·W·

READERS' COMMENTS

Please use this sheet for complaints on establishments included in the Guide or for recommending new establishments which you would like our inspectors to visit.

Please post to Egon Ronay's Guide to Lake District & Yorkshire Dales, Second Floor, Greencoat House, Francis Street, London SW1P 1DH.

N.B. We regret that owing to the enormous volume of readers' communications received each year we will be unable to acknowledge these forms, but they will certainly be seriously considered.

1987
Name and address of establishment

| |
| |
| |
| |
| |
| |

Your recommendation or complaint

| |
| |
| |
| |
| |
| |

Name of sender (in block letters)

Address of sender (in block letters)

READERS' COMMENTS

Please use this sheet for complaints on establishments included in the Guide or for recommending new establishments which you would like our inspectors to visit.

Please post to Egon Ronay's Guide to Lake District & Yorkshire Dales, Second Floor, Greencoat House, Francis Street, London SW1P 1DH.

N.B. We regret that owing to the enormous volume of readers' communications received each year we will be unable to acknowledge these forms, but they will certainly be seriously considered.

1987
Name and address of establishment

| |
| |
| |
| |
| |
| |

Your recommendation or complaint

| |
| |
| |
| |
| |
| |

Name of sender (in block letters)

Address of sender (in block letters)